TUNBRIDGE WELLS

I was born on the Pantiles

The Author was born on the Pantiles and lived in the town until she married, eventually returning to settle permanently.

She records and reminisces on past events, and mentions nearly 300 names from 1910-1990 of shopkeepers and citizens with some amusing anecdotes and much information on customs and the way of life in those days.

ISBN 0 9516715 0 2

ACKNOWLEDGEMENTS

Acknowledgement is made to the Tunbridge Wells Reference Librarians for the use of some of the illustrations in this book. My thanks also to the Kent and Sussex Courier and to the Rev. B. L. Gant of the Church of King Charles the Martyr, Tunbridge Wells.

Published and distributed by
Turney Publications
20 Mountfield Road
Tunbridge Wells
Kent TN1 1SG

Printed by Xpress Printing Services,
Crowborough, Sussex, England.

Family group, author seated on Mother's lap.

To Susan and Jane

CONTENTS

Chapter 1 Our House, 60-66 The Pantiles · Our Father · Kaiser's Bonfire · Musical Box · Ghost · Horse bolts · Stocking The Shop · Brother Impaled · Pin Swallowed

Chapter 2 Nelly's Hair Cutting · Grandma's Picnics · Father and Games · Wartime Diet · Gaslighting

Chapter 3 Cadena Café · Uncle Harry · Balloon Man · Band Playing · Woman with Horns · Great Hall · Pantiles Shops

Chapter 4 Circus · Dad in Uniform · Agricultural Show · Punch and Judy · Feet at Window · Brighton Lake

Chapter 5 Dad says Goodbye · The Fair · The School · Coconut Shies · Prizes

Chapter 6 Visit to High Rocks · School Starts · Beaters · Dad is Killed

Chapter 7 1918 · War Memorial · Grandma's Operation · Pantiles Shopkeepers · I am Ambushed

Chapter 8 Motorbike Accident · Courier Office Fire 1927 · High Street Traders · King Charles Church · Sanders and Romary's Biscuits

Chapter 9 Weekes and Great Hall Cinema to Mount Pleasant · Man's Suicide · Concert Party · My Operation · Brown's Poultry Farm · Great Storm of 1922 · Saturday Market

Chapter 10 Mount Pleasant Traders · Woolworths Opens · Drapers · Ironmongers · Chemists · Hairdressers · Carpenters · Dressmakers · Food · Clothing · H.M.V. and list of some local residents

Chapter 11 Art Scholarship · Pump Room · Popular Dogs · I Learn to Drive · Jobbing Gardener · Teeth · Dresden China · Visit to London

Chapter 12 Tunbridge Wells 1990 · Hurricane · Development · Woolworths Prices · Pantiles Today · Shopkeepers · Corn Exchange and Speyhawks · Town's Attractions

AUTHOR'S PREFACE

This book has been written as a record of what happened in my first twenty five years of life, and includes the period from just before the Great War in 1914 up to shortly before the Second War in 1939 as well as the present time. I hope the book will give an insight into the customs and ways in which people lived in those days, together with the names of shops and shopkeepers, and some of the population. Any books which I have read on Tunbridge Wells have all been early ones, from about the year 1700-1800. I feel there might be a need for someone to write something more up-to-date, so that those living at the present time may be able to look back, and enjoy the reminiscences of my day, and even find some of the names of those who lived there, or have relations who can remember them. I have mentioned about three hundred names altogether, and described the town in 1990.

My Father's death, John Gilpin Butcher's, was reported in the Courier in September 1917 as follows:- 'News has been received that Gunner J. G. Butcher R.G.A. has been killed in action in France. Mrs Butcher first learnt the sad news from a comrade of her husband who stated that he was one of a group of five amongst whom a shell burst one day last week, and they were all killed. The funeral took place with Military Honours. Mr Butcher, who leaves a widow and three young children - the youngest of whom attains her fifth birthday this week - was well known and popular in the town. He was a member of the Tradesmen's Association, and a keen sportsman, having been very successful both as an angler and a shot. Shortly before the war he had extended his business on the Pantiles, by taking another shop, and since he has been in the Army his wife has been bravely doing her best to keep the business together until such time as she hoped her husband would return. The Upholstery part of the business, in which Mr Butcher succeeded his late employer, Mr Booty, is one of the oldest on the Pantiles, and Mr Butcher was very popular among his fellow townsmen. He was aged thirty-four, and joined the R.G.A. in March of this year, and went out to France three months ago. Cheerful letters had been received from him during the last few weeks stating how lucky he had been in the big push of that period to have got through unhurt. He was in the recent heavy fighting around Ypres, and got through without a scratch, but has now met his death by a chance shell. With Mrs Butcher who will be disposing of the Pantiles business, the greatest sympathy will be felt. Mrs Butcher has received the following letter from Major Disall "It is with the deepest regret I have to inform you that your husband was killed in action on the morning of the 26th. He was killed instantaneously by a shell which burst in the battery, and it may be some small consolation to you to know that he cannot have suffered. On behalf of all ranks, I offer you our deepest sympathy in your sad loss. Your husband was buried this morning (September 27th) at Ypres Military Cemetery."

After my brother left School there was a summary of his success in the Army which read as follows: - Mr Butcher's son Claude George enlisted as a Private in the 2nd Batt. Queen's Own Royal West Kent Regiment, April 1927; Sergeant, March 1929, entered Royal Military College Sandhurst by scholarship from the ranks, September 1929, passed out 2nd out of 180 cadets, December 1930, gaining Norman Gold Medal for Senior Indian Army Cadet, Prize Sword for Tactics, 250 Scholarship; gazetted to Indian Army as 2nd Lieut; January 1931 - attached 2nd Batt. 6th Rajputana Rifles (Prince of Wales Own), March 1932; appointed Lieutenant, April 1933; appointed Quartermaster, January 1934; appointed Adjutant, September 1936, selected as Staff Officer, Indian Army Coronation Contingent, May 1937 - an honour only shared by two other subalterns in the whole of India.

My brother stayed in India until the Indian Army was disbanded, then he came back to England and was appointed Area Organizer for Civil Defence for Hampshire, then that was disbanded and he retired. He married Sir Hugh Garrett's daughter and had three children, one of whom died of typhoid in India at an early age. My brother died suddenly in his car from a heart attack ten years ago, which was very sad.

My sister firstly married a Ship Owner and had one son who is a lawyer, her second husband was a retired Doctor. Her first husband died when he was in his fifties, and she died after a stroke twenty years ago.

My first husband died when he was fifty of heart failure, and I re-married twelve years afterwards, and after six years he also died. I have a son and two lovely grandchildren who are a great joy to me, I think grandparents enjoy their grandchildren so much, because they have time on their hands and are not so busy as the Mothers, so are greatly blessed.

When you get to the end of the book you may well ask why I have not mentioned the Victoria Development, it is because it is in its very early stages and will take about two years to complete, so at present we are unable to visualise the result, so will wait and see, but change it is sure to bring, and the town centre is certain to alter, we must progress, it does not happen every year, and may be a century before it recurs - so let us look forward to its completion.

The author and her Mother.

TUNBRIDGE WELLS

I was born on the Pantiles

Josephine Butcher

Mrs Sarah Porter,
Queen of the Touters at Tunbridge Wells, 1760.

CHAPTER ONE

OUR HOUSE SHOPS AND FAMILY

I was born on the Pantiles, not literally on the Pantiles - but in a house opposite the Bandstand. It was at 8.45 a.m. and my brother was just going to school when he ran along the Pantiles - and to everyone who passed him he said "I've got a new baby sister, she's not on a picture postcard, but a real one!".

The sun was shining and it was a lovely day. All the lime trees were still in leaf although it was approaching autumn, being early October. My Father was living in a flat in Brunswick Terrace, which was in Mount Sion, Tunbridge Wells. It was a large white house at the top of a hill, overlooking the Common. My brother and sister were born there. My Father was working for Mr Booty at 60-66 Pantiles, he was a Silk Mercer and sold materials and furnishings. My Father had the chance to take over the business from Mr Booty, so in 1911 we moved into 60-62 The Pantiles and I was born there. My sister was two years old and my brother four years. My Father had very little money, and approached his Father and asked him whether he could lend him a hundred pounds to get stock for the business: but his Father, who was comfortably off said "You know what you can do my boy, you can do what I did, go and earn it, the same as I did".

The shop was large - with superb curved windows reaching high up, and right down to the ground, with a glass door in the middle, and two or three flat windows to the left, making it as large as approximately three shops. The main display part led out from the entrance and there were a few stairs up, which led towards the rear of the shop, and either side of the walls there were wooden fixtures with deep shelves so carpets and rugs could be arranged in rolls on them on display, as well as rolls of material. There were two large windows looking onto the Common and a glass door in the centre. The main road opposite was called Major York's Road, and still is. We had a workshop on the right hand corner of the road, quite a large white building in which the men used to upholster the furniture for the shop.

My Mother told me that one day a horse and cart were coming down Major York's Road when the horse took fright and bolted, rushed across the road, and ran straight into the plate glass window. Unfortunately, the horse was killed instantly.

My Mother was a beautiful girl with long wavy auburn hair right down to her waist, brown eyes and a creamy skin. She was petite, with very small hands and feet, her Grandmother had been chosen by an artist to sit for him and she had the same colouring as my Mother.

When my Mother was in her 'teens she lived at the seaside and suffered from asthma. The doctor advised her to move to an inland town - he said "If you don't, you will die". So she moved to Tunbridge Wells and lived in a Hostel. When she first met my Father he was walking along with a friend and he said to him "That's the girl I'm going to marry". She married my Father quite soon afterwards. She was very musical and played the piano expertly, mostly light opera and dance music. She was always smartly dressed and was an expert seamstress and made all her own clothes, mostly from remnants bought at sales. She was not troubled with asthma again until I was eleven or twelve years old.

My Father was a well-presented man, of medium height, with fair hair and a moustache, blue eyes and a bald head - he always wore black suits with a waistcoat and gold watch and chain - stiff white starched collars, generally white flannel shirts with a black stripe in winter. He had a bright personality, was very popular with both ladies and gentlemen, very fond of children, very quick in movement and made instant decisions. Mother used to tease him about his bald head and he always used to say to her "You can't have brains and hair too!". All the men in our family, brothers and cousins, all went bald at an early age, but were blessed with plenty of brains!

My brother had very coarse wavy hair. It was so fair it was almost albino, and a fresh complexion and chubby body and blue eyes. He had a very jolly temperament and was easy to get on with.

My sister was a fairly plain child, with hair which was very fine but dead straight. She had green eyes and rather an inward temperament.

As the shop was without stock my Father had to improvise: as he had very little money - he arranged with the wholesalers to buy short lengths of material and carpeting - and draped them over stands so that it looked as if he had whole rolls. They also let him have furniture on a sale or return basis, and Mother put a notice in the window saying "Curtains and Blinds made and lined to Order". As my Father had a very pleasant personality and a good business head, he soon found he was patronised by a lot of elderly ladies who lived in large houses in the town. We were in an expensive end of the town, with high-class shops all along the Upper Walk, and a lot of the houses above the shops had beautiful wrought iron verandahs. There was also the Bandstand at one end, and the Chalybeate Springs at the other, near King Charles the Martyr Church. So I think I was lucky to be born in such lovely surroundings.

When I was older and able to understand, my Mother told me that she hated having to go down the flight of stone steps at the rear of the shop leading to the cellar. She had to bring up a bucket of coal for the kitchen range when our maid, Florence, was off duty. Mother was afraid of mice, and as there was no light down there she was really scared, especially as one day she unknowingly shovelled up a live toad - I can remember it well, especially as I knew we three children had been down to collect newts and toads at the Brighton Lake.

Our shop extended as far along the Pantiles as the Tobacconists - next door to it was the sweet shop, Jupps. Every Easter they used to put a simply enormous chocolate egg in the window. The biggest egg I have ever seen, or think I will ever see again: it had lovely sugar flowers on it in the centre, violets, roses and daisies and foliage. Raffle tickets were on sale at three pennies each - we had to guess the weight. I believe it contained chocolates inside which would make it even harder to guess how much it weighed. The winner would have been given the egg, otherwise it would go to Tunbridge Wells Hospital. We kept buying tickets all the time, and in spite of this we never won. We never heard of anyone else doing so, so I suppose it went to the Hospital every year.

The Pump Room was across the road. We went down the steps, and at the end of the Pantiles we crossed over past the Lower Walk. The Hunt Ball was held there every year, so we used to watch the people arriving in their carriages to go to the Ball. When I grew up I was able to go to dances there. The Fairy Lights were all on, and the Pantiles looked so pretty as the lights were glass jars with a candle inside and hung up in strings between the trees and lamp posts - the Fairy Lights were made of knobbly glass, in lots of different colours.

I must tell you about our house, which comprised the hall, with a door either side, one being the side entrance and the other being the main entrance - my pram used to stand in the hall. Our house adjoined the shop premises, the Swan Hotel was next to our house.

I was a fairly ordinary looking child, I had brown eyes and brown hair and a pale skin like my Mother, but not her auburn hair. One morning Florence our maid said to my Mother "Come and look ma'am, baby's eyes are changing colour - one eye is blue and the other eye is brown". Mother said "I've been told all children are born with blue eyes and that if they are going to they change to brown later on, so that's what must be happening". The first day I had one blue eye and one brown eye when it happened, and then the next day I had both brown ones. I was the only one in the family, apart from my Mother, to have brown eyes.

In our house there was an elegant white staircase in the hall, with a mahogany hand-rail leading to the first floor. When we were older we used to slide down on these banisters and had good fun with it. Our sitting-room was a combined room, with bay windows; my parents' bedroom was above. So we had a beautiful view of the Pantiles and the Bandstand. It was when it was re-decorated that the workmen found some old bill posters on the walls advertising the Theatre - some say it was very likely a Gaming House as it was near the Assembly Rooms, or it could have been a Boarding House for guests. It was a very old building and beside the dining room there was a small room long and narrow with shelves which we called the Pantry. We kept all the office supplies for the shop in there, such as blotting paper, candles, sealing-wax and a bill hook, which always fascinated me as receipts were stuck on this with bills. It comprised a steel upright with a hook at the end, mounted on a round block of wood - one had to press the bill onto the hook and press it down to the base, when eventually it would fill up and we had to start another one. Next to this room were two or three empty rooms, they were disused and ran along the shops as far as the Tobacconists.

We used the first room as a playroom, my Father fixed a string to the ceiling so that it hung down, and my brother used to invite all his friends round to take part in the apple game. An apple was tied on the end of the string and we all had to stand in a circle, hands behind our backs, and whoever was in charge would then swing the string with the apple on it in a wide circle and as it slowed down we all tried to take a bite. I was one of the smallest ones with the shortest legs, so I never got a bite, but whoever did was made the winner and allowed to swing the apple next time. Sometimes in the dining room if my parents were out we would mark out the carpet with chalk and play marbles. We also played conkers, but I was always the loser being youngest, but remained undaunted. Leading from this room we went along to the kitchen, which was on the right hand side - we had an enormous oblong, well-scrubbed kitchen table, very like the ones they had in butcher's shops - and a large black coal fired kitchen range. Florence the maid had to clean the kitchen range which had an oven at the side. She used a housemaid's box, which was made of wood - it was oblong with a handle at the top and had a tray divided into sections to keep the brushes in. They were oval wooden handled brushes of soft bristle - there was a round one as well for corners and an oval one for putting the polish on and one for polishing, but we generally finished up with a velvet pad. The steel edges of the range and the door handles had to be done with emery paper and the ashes from the range were always sprinkled on the window boxes. In the same way we always saved the soot from the chimneys after they were swept.

We all had our meals in the kitchen, the six of us, which included

Florence who always wore uniform, and had to keep an eye on me. She was a dark-haired country girl, with jet black hair. At breakfast, I was never allowed a whole egg for myself - I didn't like the white, so they used to let me dip a bread finger into the top of my brother's and sister's eggs so I could get the yolk. They never seemed to mind.

When the Sweep came to sweep the chimneys we used to go outside and watch to see if the brush had come out of the chimney pot. You could see it sticking out in the sky and he always turned it round in a circle and gave it a shake when it was up in the air. Some people even let their chimneys go on fire on purpose to save having the Sweep and a crowd gathered outside to watch it burning. He was a very good Sweep and he used to come with a small barrow with all his brushes and things on, and his name was Mr Pavey. Everybody knew the Sweep - it was like when we played happy families with cards. We used to have Mr Bun the baker, Mrs Bun the baker's wife - well, he was Mr Pavey the Sweep. When my Father wanted his shoes cleaned he would get the Boot Black to do them. This was the man who did it professionally in the street and he had to pay him. My Father was very strict over food and insisted upon us eating our fat meat. We all three hated the fat on the edge of the meat - it really revolted us - Mother did not know what we did, but we always used to have white starched damask napkins, so when we were eating we would drop the fat onto our laps on the napkins, and afterwards go to the kitchen where the kitchen range was. There was a pipe at one side of it called the flue and we used to stuff the fat up the pipe. One day the chimney sweep came and the brush wouldn't go up, and lumps of fat eventually fell down onto the floor. He called my Mother, and she was amazed but also amused and didn't betray our secret.

After you passed the kitchen you continued along the landing, the lavatory was at the far end. It had a mahogany seat boxed in, and a handle which you had to pull up to flush the pan. It was a nice pan, it was white with blue flowers on it. We used to like sitting in there.

At the end of each day we always looked forward to our Father coming upstairs from the shop. He always came to the sitting room and got down on all fours and played bears, we used to ride on his back until eventually he shook us all off, one by one, and then rolled over onto the floor. As he did so, all the money used to fall out of his pockets, and we used to scramble for it. He always went about in a smart dark suit and wore a bowler hat and carried an umbrella. I remember asking my Mother where I had come from and so she hesitated, then she looked at me and said "Well, I found you under a gooseberry bush, of course".

Still going along the landing, there was a very small room, and it had a very short ladder with about five rungs in it, which if you climbed it led out onto the top of the building. It was a flat roof and my Mother used to dry her washing up there. My Father used to keep window boxes, and he grew tomatoes in them and he got a very good crop every year. I used to like going up there because we could see all the crows up in their nests, and hear them cawing. It was lovely looking across the common, especially if the Fair was there, which used to come periodically in the year and you could get a sort of bird's eye view of it.

My parents' bedroom was in the front of the house looking onto the Bandstand and that is where I was born. I can remember my Mother had, beside the dressing table, what she called her hair tidies. They were two little cone-shaped things made of velvet, hand embroidered with some beads on for ornamentation on the outside. When she combed her hair (it was such long auburn hair) she often had a lot of it left in the comb, and she used to screw it up into a roll and put it in these hair tidies. It saved dropping it about on the floor, I suppose it was quite a good idea. My Mother always had a silver hair brush and comb and a manicure set so that if she wanted to polish her finger nails she used some pink cream out of a dish which was called Cutex cream, rub that onto the nails first, and then she had a polishing pad which had chamois leather on it. She used to buff the nails to and fro, until they really got a shine. She also had a miniature size book with pages in it and it had compressed powder on them. If she wanted to powder her nose, if she was out anywhere, she would take this with her in her handbag, tear one of these pages out, rub it on her nose and it powdered it - actually it was a very handy thing to have. She also had a very nice silver hand mirror on the dressing table and another container which had a silver lid on it, embossed with cherubs - that was for keeping hair pins in. She used quite a lot of these and she also used to use nice tortoiseshell combs to keep her hair up when she piled it up on the back of her head; I loved watching her do her hair.

In the corner of the room there was a large jug and basin, which stood on top of a mahogany wash hand stand. Down on the ground there was a bamboo mat, and on it stood this large bucket, very pretty, it matched the jug and basin, being white with blue and yellow flowers on it. It had a wicker handle and also a lid with a hole in it and I always wondered why it was there. There were two chamber pots as well, these used to be used and when Florence came in she used to empty the chamber pots into the bucket, then take it away and empty it into the lavatory. There was a soap dish on the wash hand stand which matched the other things, and the top where the items stood was made of black marble with a white pattern on it.

Our children's bedrooms were at the back of the house - it was a very long room. I can't remember much about it really, except that we had a cat and my sister hated cats. When there was nobody looking she used to pick the cat up and stand on a chair and throw it up in the air until it dropped to the ground again. It always landed on its feet and I used to be absolutely horrified when I saw her doing that. She didn't take any notice however much I said to her. She only liked dogs, and I was very fond of cats and I think that may have had something to do with it.

One time I had been asleep, and I woke up and I had a sort of nightmare and I was crying out because I saw in the bedroom a man mounted on horseback . . . galloping along and I was quite sure it was really happening. I called out to my Mother and she came upstairs and said "Whatever is the matter?" I said "There has been a man on a horse, he was galloping" so she said "Don't be so silly, you have been dreaming". I said "I saw him" and to this day I can remember seeing him on that horse. Well, years and years afterwards I was talking about it to her and she said "There was a rumour that someone saw a ghost there, and it was a man on horseback - I only heard about it fifteen or twenty years after you woke that time, but it made me wonder if there was anything in it".

In our sitting room we had a portrait of an old lady on the wall, and I always used to look at it and wonder who she was, because it said Sarah Porter, Queen of the Touters. She was something to do with Tunbridge Wells long before. I don't really know who it was but my sister had the picture when Mother died and I always wished I'd been able to keep it.

We were a very happy family, and as children, my brother and myself got on extremely well. My sister had a very jealous disposition and as children my brother and myself were very fond of each other - I think my sister was the favourite of the family, I don't know why. I was a pretty delicate sort of child, maybe it was because I was a premature baby, and it may have been the wartime diet that I had, but I suffered from rickets and I had a hernia, and I used to have bilious attacks once a month until I was twelve years old.

We had a piano in the sitting room and my sister was allowed to play it, -my brother wasn't interested in it at all - my sister couldn't really play, but she did go for a few lessons to somebody who lived at the back of the Pantiles, she was a very nice lady called Miss Laflin - a very dark-haired lady. I can remember her now, she used to sway to and fro and throw her arms up and down when she was playing in rhythm with the music. Mother used to let my sister strum about on the piano, but I was never allowed to, ever - whenever I tried to climb on to the music seat, she always used to push me off. It was just the same with the musical box - it was a long one, almost like a coffin with a glass lid on it, and cylinder inside. It played about eight tunes, and I used to love this musical box. You had to wind it up

60 The Pantiles, our house.

JOHN BUTCHER

LATE JAMES BOOTY.

40, 60, 62, 64 & 66, The Pantiles,

Tunbridge Wells. . .

CARPET WAREHOUSE—Facing Common.

COMPLETE HOUSE FURNISHER.

CARPETS.

LINOLEUMS.

FURNITURE.

Bedsteads & Bedding,

Artistic Upholstery.

JOHN BUTCHER

TEL. 912. THE PANTILES.

62, our shop.

64, our shop.

66, our shop.

with the handle at the side and press a lever to get it to start. My sister was allowed to play this, but I was never, ever allowed, until one day when Mother was out of the room I made up my mind I was going to have a go. I got hold of the thing and wound it up, and my sister came over and tried to get me off it, and she bit me on the leg. I still stayed on in spite of it - she tried to push me off, when all of a sudden there was a searing pain, a crash, and the glass gave way. My knee went through the musical box, and blood all gushed out. I bellowed, and my sister called out "It serves you right" or something. My Mother came to see what had happened: my knee had been badly cut and had glass inside it and I had to have it stitched. I still have the scar to this day, but I don't think I really minded because I had at last succeeded in having a go at the thing after I had waited so long for it. It was just the same with her scooter, she would never let me have a ride on that, but all her friends were allowed to have one, and it didn't matter what. Even when we went to school, she wouldn't let me walk along with her - I was scared of worms, and she used to threaten me and say if I caught up with her she would throw a worm at me. I used to run along a few yards behind, whimpering the whole way, because I so much wanted to be with her and she wouldn't let me. The same with my brother, she used to get very cross with him if he said anything she didn't like. I have seen her pick up a vase of flowers and throw it at him with all the water in it; he was a very level headed sort of fellow, and his eyes would blaze, but he didn't say a word.

I got on with my brother so well, that we agreed that when we grew up we wouldn't either of us get married, we'd have a caravan, because we would not have enough money to buy a house and live in that together. But of course, it didn't come to pass.

At the back of the Band Stand there was a long fence - it was made of iron railings with spikes, with some sort of mitre at the top, all the way along. From the Band Stand it reached right along to the end of the Upper Walk. One day, my brother had gone out to play there and we were indoors, but the front door was wide open, which it often was, when we heard terrible screams coming from the Pantiles. We knew the sound of his voice, so we rushed out to see whatever was wrong. To our horror he had impaled himself on the fence. He'd been trying to climb over the wall and one of these spikes went right through the fleshy part of his leg, through his thigh. The spike was sticking out the other side - it was awful. We sent for the Fire Brigade and they came along and they drew the spike out of his leg. It was absolutely terrible, I shall always remember that. Then another thing he did was, he was in the house drawing on some brown paper with coloured chalks, and he pushed one up his nose for some reason or other. It went right up and wouldn't come down again! We were worried to death - we had to take him to Hospital and they had to scoop it out with something.

I was just as bad, because I went to bed one night and I had the toothache - I was terrified of going to the Dentist and didn't want to tell Mother. I thought I had a pip in the middle of my tooth, so I got out and had a look. On the dressing table there were some pins and I stuck a pin in, trying to scoop the pip out, when all of a sudden, as my hand wasn't very steady, I dropped it. The pin fell into my mouth and I swallowed it, so I had to confess. I went downstairs and told Mother what had happened, and she was absolutely dismayed. She said "I don't know what to do, we had better take you to Hospital, because it is dangerous with a metal thing like that, we can't have it in your stomach". So they said they'd X-Ray me, but they couldn't find anything - they said "the only thing you can do is to give her lots of bread to form a poultice inside, and you'll have to watch when she has a motion to see if she passes it". So I was watched like a hawk and nothing happened - I didn't pass it and as far as I know it is still there now! The things children get up to - honestly, its surprising!

My Father's Antique shop, 40 The Pantiles.

My Father's workshop, Major York's Road.

CHAPTER TWO

GRANDMA AND KAISER BILL

We were not allowed in the shop very often, and luckily I was blessed with a photographic memory: so going back to the age of three years I can remember standing inside the front door of the shop gazing out on to the Pantiles. It must have been at Easter-time, as I was holding a small basket with some fluffy yellow chickens made of cotton wool in it and I remember I had pulled the feet off one or two of them. There was a terrific thunderstorm in progress with a lot of vivid forked lightning. I thought it was lovely, and kept saying "pretty" whenever there was an extra bright flash. All this changed as I got older as I was caught in the worst storm in living memory when coming out of school.

My Father being so quick himself found it hard to bear when his workmen were slow, and it has been said that when they saw him coming they would get up speed and say "Look out, here comes the Boss", and he would get behind them and say "God made all creeping and crawling things". As the shop was so near the Sussex Auction Rooms, my Father used to go there to buy antiques so he could sell them in the shop. He bought a set of Chippendale dining chairs at one time which we used in our dining room. One day we were all sitting on them when he came in and said "Get up, I've just sold these". So he removed them and carried them down to the shop. He kept sample books of wall paper upstairs in the pantry for customers to choose from. Mother used to make windmills for me by cutting the paper into a square, then pointing the edges, fold them to the centre and placing a pin in the middle after finding a stick to act as a handle. They went round ever so well, especially when it was windy. On a calm day I used to run up and down fast, along the Pantiles, to make a breeze so that the sails went round. There were several seats with iron frames painted green, they held about six people, who used to sit there sometimes and eat a sandwich. Lots of young sparrows used to hop about nearby as sometimes people would drop a few crumbs for them. My Mother told me that if you wanted to catch a bird there was only one way to do it, and that was to sprinkle salt on the bird's tail. I believed her and she used to give me a paper bag with salt in it and a teaspoon, and I spent hours trying to catch one, but I never did manage and couldn't understand why. I should think people on the Pantiles must have wondered what on earth I was up to.

Sometimes we used to bowl our hoops along the Pantiles - my brother had an iron one which he guided round with an iron stick, my sister and I had a wooden one each. We used to know a girl who lived in a cottage on the edge of the Common, her name was Nelly. She was an only child and had long beautiful golden hair - she used to come over to play with us sometimes and one day, as it was early closing day, we were allowed into the back shop, and spent most of the time jumping in and out of the wall fixtures and landing on the piles of carpets. My sister had just come back from the hairdressers when short hair had become fashionable. She had been to have hers cut, and Nelly and I were very envious, so my sister said to Nelly "I can cut your hair for you if you like". Nelly was thrilled - my sister found a large pair of shop scissors and made a start. As Nelly's hair was waist length we seemed to have such a lot of hair to dispose of, and decided to use the waste paper baskets which were half full of torn up papers. We kept stuffing the hair into the baskets until we had got rid of it all - Nelly then went home.

The next morning we were getting ready for school, my sister as usual walking in advance of me, and when I passed the back of the Cadena Café, Nelly's Mother stepped out of the doorway, as she had been waiting - and said "What did you mean by cutting off my daughter's lovely hair ? If you do it again. I will call a policeman to see you". I was terrified and although I was an innocent party, could not find words to defend myself.

My parents used to go to King Charles the Martyr Church every Sunday morning to the Service, I think Mother sometimes had to stop at home, but my Father always went, and he used to take all three of us - when we were small we were all Christened there, and now I am years and years older, and I've been away from the Town and come back again, I decided I would go to that Church. There is the most beautiful font there, all made of marble with cherubs on it and columns all the way round, and I can visualise when my Father and Mother were both standing there and holding my brother and sister by the hand and I was being handed to the Vicar so that he could baptize me. It is a lovely Church and I have great pleasure in going there nearly every Sunday morning, and when I attended a Christening recently, I sat there and thought about the family, and how nice it would have been if they had all been with me today.

When we came back from Church my Father used to play a game, and we always waited for this to happen every Sunday. He used to get out a large white pocket handkerchief, tie a knot in one corner and one on the opposite corner: these represented people, one was the Father and one was the child. He would hold them up, one in each hand, so that they did the actions - he would start off and say "Father, Father, I've come to confess", and the other one used to answer - "Yes, my child, yes?" "last night I stole a piece of fish", "Yes my child, yes?" "And the cat ate it Father!" "Kiss your old Father - Kiss your old Father!" We used to love to hear this, we really did. I shall always remember it - and then another thing he did was really puzzling, for years I never understood it as I was so small, but he used to say to us - "Now you've got to find the answer to this, so listen carefully to what I have to say" he said "Sisters and Brothers have I none, but this man's Father was my Father's Son, so who was it in the mirror?". And of course the answer was, that it was himself, as he was looking in the mirror and could see his reflection - my brother and sister worked it out when they were a bit older but I could never really see it.

We used to keep silkworms, and we kept them in a cardboard shoe box. A friend of ours had some mulberry bushes in his garden, and brought us lots of leaves. Silkworms were like fat white caterpillars, with sort of hinged bodies and black legs, and they used to spin golden silk. We soon got tired of keeping them, like many other things including two puppies we bought from a small child who was standing on the Pantiles with an armful of puppies for sale, they were young Airedales. We didn't know the least thing about dogs, and they had worms. The excreta used to drop out of the dogs and the worms with it: my Mother said we would have to give the puppies away as it wasn't healthy to keep them with children. They were bound to grow to such a large size as they were Airedales in any case; so that finished that, and I've never had a dog of my own. Mother hated cats, and was afraid of them and had an allergy because of her asthmatic condition. I once found a beetle on the Common, a black beetle. It was quite a large one, and I took it home as a pet and put it in a matchbox and put some banana skin in with it. He loved that, and he ate a hole right through it from one side to the other. He lived about two or three weeks, it seemed to suit him.

Then there was Grandma - she came to live at Tonbridge when her second husband died, she wasn't a bit like my Mother, or my Mother wasn't a bit like Grandma to look at. Grandma was very tiny indeed, she was only about 4ft 3ins in height, she took size two in shoes, she used to wear a black watered silk coat with a fur collar on it which Mother made, a black tricorne hat with a hat pin and veil, sometimes a spotted one - which when she wanted to eat she had to turn back over her hat. She wore black woollen stockings, Mother knitted them on four steel needles, and we had to hold the wool in each hand, as if we were about to make a 'cats cradle', black lace-up boots, black gaberdine dress with a bodice, pleated lace collar and pockets, a white flannel petticoat, then a red flannel one, and lastly a white cotton one, all with pockets which Grandma kept her money in. She used to put it under the mattress when she went to bed, and always turned her back on me when she was counting her money. I used to try and peep round, but never succeeded in seeing how many notes she had. She adored bananas, and carried a little black cotton bag with a drawstring in which she kept the bananas. When she went out in the summer she used to use a sunshade

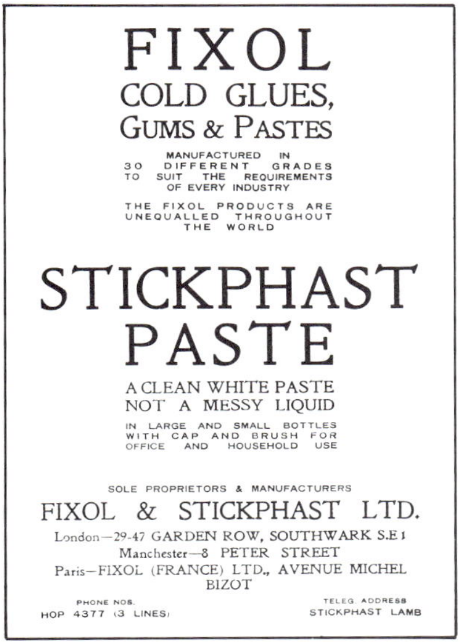

Grandma.

The Agricultural Show.

which was like an umbrella in a cream colour lined with green, and then sometimes she'd have a Japanese sunshade as well.

In the winter Grandma used to wear a snuff brown colour dress which Mother made for her, and it had a fur collar on it, she wore tall pink twill boned stays and flannel bloomers which buttoned on the sides of the legs. She sometimes wore a sealskin coat as well. She used to take me out for picnics a lot on the Common, and when we used to go we sat on a seat in the Happy Valley, and we always had jam sandwiches. She used to throw her veil back over her head to expose her face and then get out the sandwiches. Grandma hated wasps, and it was an extraordinary thing that directly she started to eat, they all came round her - and of course I was highly delighted. She was very comical, and had a good sense of humour, and would put it on rather, and shout "Oh, oh, oh" and I used to laugh and she would say "You little wretch - they're going to sting me". They never stung her but, all the same, I had a lot of fun from it. She had a passion for bananas, and we always had to take these with us, and I knew it went without saying that was what she would have, the only thing we had in common was, that we both had large appetites, she always carried a brown suede bag, and often a black cotton one with a drawstring as well. I would look at her and wonder if she had ever been young, I could only imagine her as an old lady, and thought she must have been born old, she had a large nose, and we used to tease her about this and she used to say it was very aristocratic, it was a Roman nose, but we didn't any of us inherit it. When my Father was home he was often fed up with having Grandma around so much, as she was always calling. She used to stay for so long, so Mother hit upon a solution and when Grandma was out, and my Father was in, then Mother would put a postcard in the sitting room window, and Grandma would come in and go up to her bedroom. She had a habit (even when he was out) of creeping upstairs very quietly. Mother would say "Was that the door?" I used to go and look, and Grandma would be just disappearing into her room. If I knocked she would say "Just a minute", and when I opened the door she would have her back to me. I knew she would be doing one of two things, if she had her veil up she'd be eating a banana, as she had such a passion for them, otherwise if her skirt was up, it was because she was counting her money, she refused to put it in the bank, and always carried it about with her, we never knew how many notes she had in her pocket.

Grandma used to take me for country walks, and if she saw any parsley in someone's front garden, she would knock on the front door and ask them to sell her some, she loved parsley tea, and it generally ended up by us being invited into the parlour or the back garden, and we were given tea and buns. I always knew what was coming, and I always hoped the wasps would come when she lifted her veil, but they didn't come when we were drinking tea, they only liked picnic jam sandwiches, not parsley tea. Grandma was always drinking parsley tea, she declared it was good for the kidneys. I used to go over to see her at the cottage at Tonbridge, the garden was very small. Nearly every time I went there I would walk along a narrow brick edging which she had in the garden, which got very mossy, and I always used to fall and cut my elbow. The only thing she seemed to have in the garden was mint or chrysanthemums.

Grandma was very fond of cats, and when my brother was home from school in the holidays he put a black kitten through her letter box. She kept that cat for fourteen years and wouldn't go away on holiday because of it, except once, when we took a furnished house in St Leonards, but she refused to come because of the cat, she called it Blackie. One day we looked out of the window and who should be coming along the road but Grandma, the cat was writhing about in her black cotton bag. She'd got tired of living on her own, so decided to join us.

Soon after her seventy-second birthday she came in one day and said to Mother in front of us "I'm thinking of getting married again", this was a bombshell - we said "Grandma, you can't, you're over seventy" she said "Well, what of it, I'm lonely". So Mother said "Who is it, and when did you meet?" she replied "We met in the Park, he's a bachelor, eighty years old and lives in a cottage in a town about three miles from here. He's proposed, and said 'Would I marry him?' ". Shortly after that they were married, and she went to live in his cottage. He was a good husband, and he always got the breakfast and laid the fire every morning, even on the day he died, which was about six months afterwards. Grandma's Christian names were Emily Frances, and her first husband died when he was fifty-four - he was walking along one day, carrying an umbrella and suddenly noticed that he couldn't feel his hand, and he hadn't the umbrella any longer - he had had a stroke and he simply died within twenty-four hours. It was a tragedy.

To go back to the Pantiles - of course War was declared on 4th August 1914. My Father wasn't called up straight away, because they knew he had a business to run, and he had only really started it as he was only thirty years of age at that time, but it affected us in various ways as people didn't spend so much money in buying things in the shop. Also food became very scarce, we had strange things to eat, we used to have a great block of stuff called honey sugar, I really didn't know what it was made of, but it tasted very sweet (rather like honey). We used to spread it on our bread, another thing we used to have was bread and dripping - when the meat was cooked and the dripping was left over we ate it on our bread, that was probably what made me so bilious. We used to like the dark jelly - the part at the bottom of the basin - I wouldn't dare eat anything like that nowadays.

I well remember Florence one day rushing into the kitchen to tell us that someone had seen a Zeppelin above the Common. So we ran along to the small room where the ladder was, so that we could get up on to the roof, when lo and behold there it was, up in the sky, like a silver ship looking down at us, it was the only time I ever saw a Zeppelin but I well remember it. Incidentally, Florence was carrying me and she tripped in the excitement and dropped me, and the scar on my head has been there ever since.

Another thing we did was, as we knew the family had gone out, we decided to light a bonfire, and burn the Kaiser on it. He was known as Kaiser Bill, so we gathered up all the rubbish we could find, and we went up on to the roof where the tomatoes and things were kept, it was a flat lead roof. I remember holding up my skirt and tipping out all the paper from the wastepaper baskets on to it, then pinching the corners together and climbing up the ladder to empty it out on to the roof. We'd got a bag and made it into a Guy, put it on top of the bonfire, and then we set fire to it - it burnt very well. After a little while there was much black smoke and it was getting very hot up there, and what had happened was, we had set fire to the lead on the roof and it started to melt. We panicked and knew we had set the roof on fire, so we had to rush down and tell the men in the shop what had happened, and they had to send for the Fire Brigade. We thought we'd get into terrible trouble with my Father when he came in, but he was quite nice about it, and was highly amused by the fact that we were burning this effigy of the Kaiser, much to our relief!

We had a lovely large rocking horse in our Nursery, a dapple grey, with real hair and it used to really rock, it would be very valuable today.

In those days we mostly had gas for lighting in the house, and they had glass lampshades usually, and there was a brass rod hanging from the ceiling with a bar across and hanging down each end was a chain with a handle to pull the light 'on' and 'off' with a glass globe in the middle, a gas radiant or wick was in the middle. We used to use gas fires, and we had to light those, and my sister hated doing them, as when we turned the gas on, it used to build up very quickly, so that when we applied the match the gas ignited with an awful bang. She used to be so nervous when she was lighting it, that she used to drop the match before it reached the fire, and then of course had to start all over again, when even more gas had escaped. The street lights were lit by gas, the man used to go along the Pantiles at night to put the lights on or off, and he had a long pole with a double head at the end - we called him Learie the Lamplighter.

CHAPTER THREE

THE BALLOON MAN AND PANTILES SHOPS

Grandma was delighted to have two girls and one boy as grandchildren as her other daughter had emigrated to Australia and the third one married a poor ne'er-do-well and although they had three daughters, my Mother was Grandma's favourite and it was only at the end of her life that she spent alternate months with my Aunty Cis.

Grandma used Thermogene in the winter, it was like orange coloured cotton wool, and she used to put a square of it on her chest and declared that if it was worn next to the skin it would keep bronchitis away. She always washed her hair in rainwater, and for supper had bread and milk, and she would use a bread poultice if she cut her finger. Her spare clothes were kept in a large cardboard box with camphor balls, they had the most nauseating smell which I can recognise anywhere: she said they kept the moths away. If we had colds she used to rub our chests with camphorated oil, this had a very pungent smell and the fumes made our eyes water. In wet weather she wore galoshes over her shoes, they were made of rubber, and slipped over the top of the shoes making them waterproof. Another thing she did was always to carry in the small pocket of her red flannel petticoat a small potato (uncooked), it became very shrivelled in time, and she would take it out of her pocket if we asked to see it, and when we said "Grandma, what's the potato for?" she used to reply "I keep it in my pocket to prevent me from having gall stones". We didn't know what gall stones were, but accepted the explananation without question.

She used to love to visit us and take a look at the shops along the Pantiles - my favourite shop was along the far end and near the Springs - the grown-ups always referred to the Springs as the Chalybeate Springs, but we called them the Springs. One person when asked how to pronounce the name said "Why, Charley-be-arty, of course!". Porters' toy shop was my favourite because I loved lots of dolls and Mother used to make wonderful silk dresses for them, hats and coats, and even shoes and socks. The dolls were very large and made in Germany with lovely hair. In Porters' shop they had shelves with spare dolls heads for sale, as they were made of porcelain and they broke very easily. The wigs were made of real hair - from blonde to brunette. As I often dropped my doll when running along the Pantiles Mother used to send me to Porters to choose a new head, and a new wig, and they used to fix it on the doll for me whilst I waited. It was a lovely large toy shop with a huge stock of toys.

My brother was very naughty one day as he used a lot of sticky paper which came off the sides of postage stamps and stuck lots of pieces of this paper on all of Porters windows - I don't think they ever found out who put it on the windows as we didn't hear anything about it.

We used to play with our spinning tops and whips on the Pantiles and were very fond of skipping too. My brother's favourite shop was Maynards sweet shop which was very near our house - next door to the Swan Hotel. One day our rich Uncle, my Father's brother, who was an Auctioneer in London, came down to see us - in Maynards window they had a large display of chocolate creams. The window was nicely dressed, with a red satin cloth as a base, the only thing on display was a huge pyramid of these choclate creams, it was to persuade people to buy them. My Uncle took my brother along to the shop, pointed to the sweets and said "Would you like some?". My brother was delighted and they went inside and the Assistant filled up a bag with about a pound of chocolate creams and passed them over to my Uncle - when they got outside, Uncle Harry offered my brother one - he burst into tears and got into a terrible rage - threw the bag of sweets on to the ground and jumped on them and said "Those are not the chocky creams I wanted - I wanted THOSE chocky creams" and he pointed to the tall pyramid in the window, he thought he was going to have the whole lot! Poor Uncle Harry!

We used to buy our sweets at Maynards, we didn't have much pocket money 1d or 2d a week, so we always looked for value for money, aniseed balls at eight a penny used to be the best. Gob-stoppers were large, ball-shaped, hard as a bullet and almost tasteless, but if you sucked them for a while they changed colour, so we were constantly taking them in and out of our mouths to see what colour they were. We also bought peppermint humbugs, brown and white, these were giant size with triangular sharp edges, and very difficult to eat without dribbling as our cheeks were completely distended, and child-like we used to try and make each other laugh when we were sucking them, by pulling faces at each other. We used to buy sherbert dabs, which were packets of sherbert on a stick, and we sucked the end, it had the effect of sherbert responding by coming down our noses in some peculiar way. My Mother's favourite was a Fry's whipped cream walnut or a bar of Fry's chocolate cream, they were about 2d each. I remember buying for 3d (which was a lot of money in those days for a child) a surprise packet - they had sweets made of sugar, very hard and dry, pale pink or cream, in the shape of crescents or circles. When you bit them sometimes there would be a prize inside, the best prize being a sixpence - we kept buying them hoping to get a sixpence, but we got a lucky charm instead like we had in Christmas puddings, until one day I actually found a sixpence in mine, I shall never forget how delighted I was. So of course I went back and bought some more and used my sixpence that way without any further results, so I lost my money. 'We learn the hard way.'

Edinburgh rock was very nice especially the raspberry and ginger kind, and we had liquorice pontefract cakes, they were very cheap too. My Mother was fond of gelatine lozenges, which were extremely thin and lasted a long time when they were eaten. At Christmas we always had chocolate sugar mice with white eyes and long tails, and sugar pigs made of icing sugar; very sickly, we were not keen on those.

Just past Maynards there was a fur shop, people used to buy fur coats there, and if they got tired of them they could have them cut short and then they looked like a new coat: after all, the War was on and we had to economise. Further along, there was the Hand and Sceptre Hotel, but I think it was called Parker and Hammicks, or else it could have been next door to it, there was a small iron railed gate and at the end - there was a grotto with water dripping down. There were yellow tiled walls, and past the grotto at the end they once had an Exhibition there, a large picture of Christ, with a luminous halo above it, painted by a man named Butler. They had a black curtain behind it and people left coins in a saucer after viewing the picture.

Then there was an Optician's shop, Mr Sturt the Optician was in charge - the Cadena Café was on the same side and always had a clock hanging on the wall outside. It was a large Restaurant, and it extended to the rear looking on to the Common. In the front shop they had cakes to choose from for tea or coffee, and people used the downstairs for this. Upstairs they had a Restaurant for luncheons, all the waitresses wore brown cotton uniforms with cream muslin frilled aprons - collar, cuffs and caps matching with a thin brown velvet bandeau across the front. Round their waist a belt with a small booklet of bills and a pencil, so that they could write down the order and then tear the page out afterwards and present the bill. They had an Orchestra which played every day with a grand piano and two violinists - it was a nice meal, three-course, soup, joint and two vegetables, pudding and coffee for 1/9d. Today that would be nine pence all told! We went there twice a week when I was older - but not when we were living on the Pantiles.

Boots the Chemists was next door to the Springs and had a large Lending Library upstairs. As children we used to drink the water from the Springs - you first of all opened the iron gate near Boots, went down the steps, and there was an iron chain on the left hand wall with an iron cup attached hanging on a hook. We would lift the chain off the hook, dip the cup in the well, and drink as much as we wanted. We hated the taste of the water as it was rather like ink, but got used to it as time went on. The lady who served the waters was called a Dipper and she was very tall and wore a black dress and bonnet - but when I was older there was another lady there instead, long dresses were not worn at that time: they were both very nice ladies. There were iron chairs for people to sit on to drink the water, green chairs with slatted seats which folded up, so that at the end of the day the Dipper would store them away in the tiny room where she used to wash the glasses. Some people went there every day when they were on holiday, because they knew that Queen Victoria used to go there and it was supposed to be very good for one.

There was a Post Office on that side of the Walk near Porters, but it moved along later to No. 40 after my Father had it for Antiques. There was another sweet shop called Harringtons, they made their own sweets. Fox Brothers was at the end and sold ladies' clothes. Outside Charltons the Florists they had a rain measuring gauge in a glass case mounted on wooden legs, it may have given the weather as well, I am not sure. Across the road on the corner there was a very large high class shop called Dusts, it sold lovely clothes and linen, they had beautiful things in it, hats and gloves, bags and shoes, to mention a few. Then there was a Tailors called Mercers, and they made gentlemen's suits. Durrants the Grocers came next, a wonderful Grocers with a young man who was so very polite, he always remained cheerful however busy he was or however difficult the customers were. I really think he helped to make the business as he was so good, we used to buy rusks and cracknel biscuits and Bath Olivers there, as well as crystallised fruits. Ashby the Butcher was next, and the men who were serving used to wear straw hats, long blue and white aprons, and sometimes white coats. They had pheasants, rabbits and hares hanging up above their window on steel hooks, and there was always a lot of sawdust on the floor. White paper bags were hanging up with a piece of string through one corner, they had pigs, sheep and cows, I think, hanging up, but no fur on them. The only ones with the heads left on seemed to be the pigs, they were hanging head first downwards with their heads in a bucket. There was a large, very thick wooden table on one side of the shop and the butchers used to chop everything up on it, with very sharp knives and axes. There was a lady who took the money and she was in a tiny room with a glass window and a shelf at the bottom - we used to put the money on it when we bought meat.

I think there was a Bootmaker called Collins next door who repaired riding boots, and even made shoes sometimes. There was Biggs, the Wine and Spirit/Grocers shop. In the Fishmarket Mr Tolson used to have lots of fish spread out on a slab with ice in between, and when we wanted ice for ice cream we used to take a bucket along and get some ice from him, and hurry home quickly so the ice wouldn't thaw. We used to put the ice into a wooden churn and turn the handle round and round to make the ice cream.

Charltons the Florists came next, and they sold seeds and plants, flower pots and flowers. We were at School with their daughter as far as I can remember, and I think their Father married twice and was keen on dancing. Kemp, the Antique Dealer came next, he spent a lot of time at the Auction Rooms and was an expert at buying and selling, their daughter married Mr Strawson - he worked in the shop. He was a tall man with pink cheeks and blue eyes, I think he had an Adam's apple as well. Their motto was 'Our word is our bond' and I always admired them for it when I was older, as I knew it meant that they would never go back on their word: I have tried to copy it. They had a storage place next door to the saleroom at the Corn Exchange, and it was crammed full of such beautiful things for sale, from teenage I used to go there a lot to admire everything.

Recently I came across my Father's telephone number in a Directory, and as he was killed during the War, I've very few memories of him as I was so young, but seeing this number brought it home to me more than words can say. I realised what I'd lost, having to be brought up without a Father, my reaction was to say "Please God, can I phone my Father in Heaven?" But to no avail - how sad - what I have missed ....

I remember two other things about the Pantiles, one was that there used to be a balloon man when the Band was playing there, and he always stood in the gap just between Maynards and the Fur shop where there is an open path with steps up, beside the Swan Hotel. The balloon man was a nice man, just like Father Christmas to look at, he had white hair and a white beard, and a very pleasant face always smiling, and he had an enormous cotton bag and all the balloons were kept inside it, you can imagine the size it must have been! He used to stand there holding up whole strings of balloons in the air, and he had different prices, most of them ld or 3d each, but the largest were 6d each. I used to have one sometimes, but never one of the really large ones as they were too expensive and we couldn't afford them. One day I was standing there, very enviously looking at these balloons, when a gentleman came along with a small girl, and bought her one of these big ones. He turned to me and said "Would you like a balloon, little girl ?" so I said "Yes, please". So he picked me out one of the huge ones and I was simply delighted. I shall always remember how pleased I was, I rushed home to show it to my Mother - she was furious - she said "Where did you get that from?" I said "a man bought it for me". She said "What sort of man - you know I've told you not to talk to any man" I said "Well, he was with a little girl, he bought her one and asked me if I'd like one, so I said I would". And when she was reassured, then all was well - it turned out to be a gas filled one, I don't know how he managed to get it into the balloon but suppose he had a pump or something, and that's why it was dearer, and so much bigger - I had at last got my hearts- desire.

The other incident was, that once I was going along the Pantiles and near the end I could see a crowd had gathered, not a large crowd, about fifteen people, and they were outside the Jewellers shop, so I asked somebody what it was, and they said "Oh, it's the lady with horns, she's in the shop buying something". Well we had heard that there was somebody living in Tunbridge Wells in an expensive area up near the Common who had actually got horns on her head, and it seems she was down in this shop and had gone there to buy something. I went along all agog and curious, and waited for her to come out - I can remember this most distinctly - she came out, she had a very pale face, she was a teenager I suppose or she might have been a bit older, because at that age it was hard for me to judge. She had a hat on - it was enormous . . . and there were two bulges, one on either side, sticking up in the air, and the hat was like a mob cap. There was a frill all around it which hung down to her shoulders and there was a blue ribbon band put round the centre to keep it on, and these two things sticking up in the air were covered up. The hat was made of white muslin and lined, because you couldn't see through it, and I'm absolutely certain that she had got horns, when she came out people melted away. I have recently met three people who also saw her.

I do remember years afterwards when someone wrote to the paper and said "Does anyone remember the woman with horns?" but I didn't reply to the letter. But I actually saw her, and it was an unforgettable experience. I was very sorry to think that she had to be like that, I'm absolutely positive she had horns.

I think my Mother must have had quite a job looking after all three of us, as it was so hilly in Tunbridge Wells and when she had to go out it was all uphill from the Pantiles to the Five Ways, especially the Wells hill; it was the worst of the lot. When you got up near the top of it, it got more and more steep, and I used to be in the pram, it was one of those high prams. It was called a Marmet pram. My brother was walking on one side holding on to Mother's hand, and my sister was hanging on to the handle of the pram, and Mother said she used to stop two or three times as it was so steep, and she was quite exhausted and said her lungs were going like bellows - especially as she was asthmatic. Mother always used to say that she never wanted to live anywhere else but Tunbridge Wells, as she loved it; and I used to say the same.

CHAPTER FOUR

THE BAND · CIRCUS · AGRICULTURAL SHOW

There were two performances a day from April to September, they were well attended, and if people didn't want to pay they used to sit on the long seats, some of which were on the left hand side of the Bandstand. The rest of us were on the right hand side, and reached along as far as the Pantiles. As there were lime trees overhead, they shed sticky stuff as the leaves got coated with it, and it used to drop onto the seats, but only for about a week or two in the summer. The main seats were in rows, from the front of the Swan Hotel, and reached to the Bandstand. If there were a lot of people the Attendant would add more chairs, as he kept a stack of them covered over with a tarpaulin in case of rain. They were canvas arm-chair style as well as some small green slatted chairs which folded up like the ones used at the Springs when taking the Waters. A season ticket could be bought, so that it allowed people to attend every performance at a cheap rate for the season - Mother always had one, as she loved music.

The Bands were all different kinds, but the most popular were the Guards' Bands, we used to like their colourful uniforms, and sometimes they would ask one of the men to sing a solo. I liked the xylophones and the trumpets, but I preferred piano music most of all, and enjoyed it when J.H. Squire arrived with his Celeste Octet. We were not keen on the Scottish Bands, they used to do a sword dance, I always hoped they would step on a sword and fall down, so that I would be able to see whether they had anything on under their kilts! Lots of people used to gather under the Colonnade, standing up, and there was constant movement all the time with people going to and fro along the Pantiles. The Sweet Shop did a trade with ice creams and chocolates, so did the Cadena Café with teas. I remember once when the Band played their Regimental March at the end of the programme, as was usual, and then followed on with the National Anthem, one man remained seated in his chair with his hat still on, whereas all the other men were standing up, with hat in hand. A man in the row behind him bent over - and with his walking stick he put it underneath the hat brim, and tilted the hat, so that it fell down into the man's lap.

There was a man called Jock, who had a wooden leg and used to limp, and he collected money for the tickets in an oblong box, which was probably mahogany, it had a thick stick-like handle on the middle of one side at the bottom, so that he could hold it with one hand.

We slept in the front of the house in the summer, and couldn't get to sleep because of the Music, so we got some farthings, covered them with silver paper, put one under each chair leg, and then removed the coin from under the leg, and it looked just like a sixpence. We used to drop them down from the bedroom window on to people's heads, and when they picked them up, they all thought they were sixpences! Mother told us that one evening she heard a lot of laughter outside, just below our window, and went downstairs to see what it was all about, people were all smiling and pointing up to our bedroom window. No wonder, as all three of us were lying on the bed, and had placed our feet flat on the window pane, so that from outside, six pink feet could be seen pressed against the glass!

I think the Band made us quite musical, and we got to like it, as when we grew up, we all liked music very much. Not only that, you see, my Mother could play the piano very well, and from my smallest days we used to tap dance to the tunes when she was playing. That was fine, because later on, when the Fair came as well, we had all the Hurdy-Gurdys' organs going on the Common. Although that was a different sort of music, when it played at the same time as the Band you've no idea how discordant it sounded all mixed up together, because we had the windows open, so you got the Band in front and the Fair at the back, it was the most ghastly noise you've ever heard!

The war had been on for quite some time now, and my Father was very worried because he had just got his business nicely started, he was in his early thirties, and it had been a great effort to get it on its feet. He didn't see how he could go off and leave it when he had been in complete charge of it, and Mother had three young children. He said "I think I will have to go, the only thing I can do, is put a Manager in, but whether it will be the same or not, I don't know, but I feel I must go". So he enlisted, and in due course he got his Army uniform and went off to collect it, and when he came back he stood in the doorway in the kitchen. My Mother looked at him and absolutely shrieked with laughter, she said she'd never seen anything so funny in her life - because he'd got very thick legs, and they wore puttees in the Army. They were like pieces of khaki braid or bandaging, and they were wound up his legs, and it made them look tremendously fat, and being fairly short and chunky, honestly he looked awful, she couldn't stop laughing. He said "What are you laughing at?" She said "Well, you look so funny", so he said "Well, I can't help it, this is what I've got to wear", so that was that. He went off, and was gone I think, about six months, and then he was wounded, I can't remember the details as I was so small, but they sent him to Bexhill, I can remember that, and we had a snapshot of him and all the men in hospital there. Because they were wounded they wore bright blue serge suits with a red tie, maybe it was a Red Cross Hospital, I haven't really thought about that. He was there for quite some time convalescing, and then he had to go back again to the Front, I will tell you more about that later on.

Lord John Sanger used to bring his Circus to Tunbridge Wells sometimes, and it was held on the Common across the road, where they had the Fairground. I very much wanted to go to it one day, but Mother said she couldn't afford it, as it was a shilling to go in, and money was short in Wartime. I tried hard to persuade her, we were sitting on the Common on a wooden seat near the Circus, and whilst we talked, I kept moving the toe of my shoe to and fro in the sandy dust, where our feet rested, all of a sudden, I kicked something. There, believe it or not, shining and gleaming in the sun, was a silver coin. I picked it up, and it was a shilling: it's a very happy memory, and it was quite by chance that I found it, because my Mother didn't drop it, as we were just sitting talking. I was able to go to the Circus after all.

Circuses haven't changed much over the years, and all the animals were on view in a small Zoo before, and after, the performance. What we liked best of all was the Band, which was a brass one. All the Bandsmen were dressed in very colourful outfits, there was a large Marquee with lights overhead and outlining the doorway where the Performers entered. The Band always began by playing the March of the Gladiators, and as all the Clowns rushed in, they were doing somersaults and cartwheels and tumbling about. Then the Grand Master entered - looking very smart in a black suit with tail coat, and holding a long whip which he cracked now and again. The usual acts of elephants and tigers took place, but I liked the Fire Eaters who swallowed fire; and then they had a lady who was fired from a cannon, she really was, and there was a very expectant hush before it was fired. I was nauseated when the snake charmer arrived, she came in, and opened up a basket, and took out a large python, and let it wind round her body right from her waist, up to her head. I've never liked snakes, and that's why I remember this happening. The custard pie acts were very amusing, and next, they announced that they were going to saw a lady in half! They brought in a box like a coffin, it was up on a stand, and she had to lie in the box and wait to be sawn in half, you can imagine how we all felt. The saw made an awful noise, we nearly died of suspense - at last the box was in two pieces, cut through the middle in half, and to our amazement the lady was still in one piece, and not cut in half, much to everybody's relief.

The performing dogs were very nice, because they came in, one of them had a pram, and she was standing up on her hind legs, and pushing the pram and there were two dogs inside dressed up as babies, with bonnets and gowns on. The Mother pushed the pram right round the ring for everyone to see, it was lovely, and everyone clapped. I don't think Lord John Sanger was a real Lord, someone said he was christened Lord, and he had a sad end, rumour had it that he was attacked by one of his animals, or one of his men, and died soon afterwards, we never found out which it was.

We used to feed the elephants afterwards when we went outside to the Marquee. If it was very hot weather, the Keepers would squirt water over them to cool them down, there were some camels as well and a white llama, very like a camel, which was white instead of fawn and didn't have a hump. We always looked forward to the Circus coming, and beforehand they used to put on a procession through the town to advertise it, so they came along with clowns all banging on drums, and trumpeters playing tunes, and crowds would gather to see them arrive. We had a good view from our windows at the back of the Pantiles, it succeeded in making all the children ask their parents to take them to see the Circus!

We had the Agricultural Show every year - we called it the Cattle Show. They had a Flower Show as well, held on a different day. The Cattle Show was held in Eridge Road, it was marvellous, all the pigs were specially washed and polished, and the sheep were shampooed and put in pens to be judged. If they won a prize, a rosette was pinned on their pen. There were some enormous pigs called sows if they were female, and some of them had about twelve piglets. There were bulls, which were led by a man with a pole, the bulls having a ring in their nose so the man could control the bull if he got angry, by putting the pole in the ring. They had to walk round to be judged, there were all sorts of animals, people all sat round the ring on a seat which was like a plank of wood on a stand. As well as goats there were rabbits, birds and chickens. They had more than one ring, people who had ponies and carriages, some were called Traps and Pairs, and dog carts, used to drive round and round. Both ladies and gentlemen wore bowler hats. The Shetland ponies were beautiful, they were so small, and had very fat stomachs and long manes and tails.

Then they had jumping competitions, for grown-ups and their horses. The winners were given rosettes to pin on the horses' harness. I used to like the cart horses as they paraded round. They had lots of brasses on their harness, and the brass on top of their heads was called a flier; their manes were all plaited with ribbons, their tails as well, and their feet had very thick hair like a fringe round the ankles. They picked up their feet so proudly as they went round the ring - pulling their carriages behind them, and people used to clap, they looked so nice.

We went to see men milking the cows, and we liked that, as we had never seen it before. As we lived so near we would spend the whole day there, it always seemed to be sunny weather. When it got too hot the ladies used to put up their sunshades, they were made of cream cotton lined with green to keep the sun out. At the end of the day there was a lot of milk left over as the Farmers had to milk the cows, and they didn't know what to do with it. If you went down there and took a jug you could stand and the

Farmer would fill it up as he milked the cow. It was beautiful, all creamy and warm. I remember we took a jug one year as we had seen other people doing that, and the milk was simply delicious.

They always had a Band and it was like a Military Band, very nice, and there were lots of people walking about, and we used to meet our friends. All that is gone now, of course, as they sold the ground and used it for housing. They put up two Council Estates there and so, if you want to go to an Agricultural Show you have to go a long way to Ardingly, which is near East Grinstead. It is a long way for Tunbridge Wells people to go to see it, we thought the Show would be held in Tunbridge Wells for ever. Mind you, it has done a lot of good by providing all those houses which were so very much needed. The Nursery is still near it, whereas it was Charltons it is now Coblands.

A lot of our time was spent on the Common, so we got to know every inch of it. We used to climb trees, I hardly ever managed it as I was so small, the trees were very tall and the branches high up, so I couldn't get started. My sister was not good at it either, but my brother was, we were not supposed to climb them, and always kept a look out for the Common Ranger. He used to be about collecting rubbish, he carried a sack and a long pole with a spike on the end of it, and he used to spear any pieces of rubbish such as paper bags with the spike, and then put the rubbish into his sack. In summertime the gorse often caught fire, as people sometimes left pieces of broken glass about from bottles. When we saw the black smoke rising we used to rush from the house, and find long pieces of bracken and use the sticks to help beat the flames out.

We used to play Rounders and French Cricket, and sometimes Horsemen whereby my brother would put a long piece of string under my armpits and tie it on, to act as reins; then he would give them a tug and say "Gee up, Horsey", and we would run fast, all along the Common mainly along the Racecourse. There was a lovely glade near there, surrounded with trees and screened from view, we used to have picnics there, it was often carpeted with golden buttercups, they used to take my breath away, it was so beautiful. There was a wooden summer house near the Higher Cricket Ground and the Queen's Grove, we used to play in that.

One winter the Brighton Lake froze over, which was most unusual, so we decided we would go skating, I don't know where we managed to get the skates from, but all three of us had some, and there was an island in the middle and so we decided to skate over to that. We had always wanted to get on that, it was in the morning - we went back again in the afternoon, and of course meantime, in the afternoon the sun had worked round and had got on to the water. It thawed the ice, and we didn't realise it, we did notice that there was water on top of the ice. My brother was the first one to get on it, and as he was the heaviest as well, there was a loud crack, the ice gave way and he fell in. It was fairly shallow where he was, and he managed to get out all right; but we were afraid to skate on it any more, in fact we warned everyone not to go on it, or they would be drowned.

In winter we used to go to the Common with our toboggans, they were wooden ones long enough to take two or three people, and had steel runners underneath. We used to get the runners put on by the Blacksmith as he had a place on the Common not far from us. We would take the sledge to the steepest part of the Common called the Donkey Ride, and my brother and sister went on our sledge, but I was too scared to go, and my hands were so cold, they felt as if they would drop off. I often ran home crying with the pain.

We liked going to the Brighton Lake and often took a drink from the Spring which came out of the wall, which was behind the lake, where there was a seat - the brickwork was stained orange from the iron water, we had to cup our hands to act as a container when we wanted a drink. We were very fond of taking a jam jar down to the lake to see what we could find, and from time to time we took home all sorts of things. We had tadpoles and frog-spawn, that was horrible looking, and things called effets, they were very funny little things, and frogs and toads and goodness knows what. Mother had to put up with all these things, I think we mostly took them down to the cellar at No. 60. I remember one particular time, we got a toad, it was a yellow spotted one, we put it in a jam jar, and we put the baby one in another jam jar, and took them home. We went downstairs with them, and as we thought the big one would be lonely, we put the baby one in with it, it was a tight fit in the jar. The next morning we went down to see how they were getting on, and there was the big one in the jar, but the baby one wasn't there: we couldn't understand it. We looked all round - it was very dark down there, and we couldn't see very well. Then we noticed that the toad had a bulge in one side, and - to our horror - we realised (as you could almost see the shape of it) that the baby one had been swallowed by the big one, and was inside the toad and you could practically see it breathing in there. Oh, it was the most awful sight, it really was, I don't know what we did with it, we had to bring it upstairs. I remember that, because Mother would have had a fit if she had seen it.

After we had taken the toad up on to the Common, and we were on our way home we went down to the front of the Pantiles and there was a Punch and Judy Show on. We loved that, to watch Punch and Judy, and his crocodile with the string of sausages and Punch hitting Judy and the Policeman coming along with a truncheon, and the way they talked to each other. We used to mimic the voices when we went in, and we loved it. They always wore the same clothes and it was the same man each year. He was very good, I think we really thought it was taking place, there were curtains on the stage which opened in the middle when the performance started, and these figures appeared. We never saw anybody else, and of course the man must have been standing underneath - making all these speeches, and taking the part of Punch and Judy. We didn't realise that, we thought it really was Punch and Judy doing it, and we loved to see the sausages and the baby as well, it made our day.

They had chestnuts for sale as well on the Pantiles that afternoon, they sold them in colder weather, and we would stand beside the fire where the man was roasting the chestnuts, and warm our hands. The chestnuts were done up in brown paper bags, I think they were 3d a bag. They were a bit black where they had been on the open fire, and we used to sprinkle some salt on them and we enjoyed them so much; they were without shells, so were easy to eat.

When we went indoors we found Grandma there, she had brought some water glass because we wanted to pickle some eggs. We had a large brown crock, it had a wooden lid with a handle across it all made of wood. We mixed this stuff up, and when it was put into the crock after being mixed with hot water, it set like a white jelly and we had to put all the eggs into this jelly to preserve them. When you wanted one, you just spooned one out of the crock, it was horrible looking stuff, but it seemed to keep all the winter through. Florence was cleaning the knives; we had a knife sharpener which was a round wooden flat-sided affair with a handle, and it had two slots on top so you could insert the long steel knives. If you turned the handle it sharpened the blades, but for cleaning purposes Florence used a long wooden board and sprinkled some brown powder on it and rubbed the knives up and down on it, very fast, and that cleaned them. When she did the ironing she had some flat irons and put them on the kitchen range to heat - using them alternately - and she always used to hold them up to her face to see if they were hot enough. She put a blanket on the table and would iron on top of that. We had a very tall Nursery fireguard, it had black criss-cross wire all the way round it, and a brass rail at the top and a flat piece of iron at the bottom. It fitted close to the fire and we sometimes used to hang the washing all the way round on it, to dry. We had bellows for when we wanted to light the fire to start it off, and they were foot ones. You pressed with your foot on these, they were big ones with leather bellows, wooden outside, studded, and with a brass ferrule. When pressed it blew hard and created a draught, and made the fire light quickly.

When it was quiet in the kitchen sometimes we would look up, and there would be a mouse sitting in one of the shoes; we had a lot of mice there, but we didn't mind. Mother didn't like them, but they seemed to stay away when she was there.

Although I have so many memories about living there, the one thing I can't remember is having a bath. I'm sure we must have had one, probably one of those very high deep ones, because if we hadn't we would have had to bath in front of the fire in a bath tub but we didn't have one of those, so we must have had a proper bath.

We did quite a few things to amuse ourselves, before we went to bed we played snakes and ladders, and ludo, and when I was a little older, draughts. I wasn't very good at that, my brother liked dominoes but he was very, very keen on soldiers and always declared that he was going to be a soldier when he grew up: which of course he was. He had a Fort with a drawbridge, it was a very nice fort; we got it from Porters Toy Shop. He had a lot of Regiments, about five or six different ones. He liked to line them all up in rows, and then he got me to play with him, and I had to be the enemy and storm the Fort. Some of the soldiers were lying down ones, with rifles in their arms, and some were standing up. Mother made a large quantity of small sandbags so that he could barricade the Fort all the way round to keep off the attack. I used to like it, as I liked the companionship, as we got on so well. My sister spent her spare time in making a scrap-book, and we would get a bottle of paste which had a brush provided with it, and it was only 3d a bottle, it was called Stickphast. Another thing we did was to make paper chips, by cutting up old pieces of wallpaper into very small pieces, and we would sit for hours cutting up these tiny pieces and filling a basin with them, we were also shown how to make paper men. We would get some newspapers and fold them into three or four layers thick, and then cut them with a pair of scissors. We then cut out the shape of a man with arms and legs, and cut away the surplus newspaper, then undo them. As they were four layers thick, they came out in long strips and were quite attractive. My sister liked knitting, but I was not any good at it, and have never been able to knit.

The Open-Air Swimming Pool.

CHAPTER FIVE

OUR FATHER SAYS FAREWELL

Schooltime - my brother went to school at St John's, Tunbridge Wells, he had to wear school uniform, and my sister went to the County School for Girls which was quite near Skinners, Miss Hughes was the Headmistress. They went by bus from the Pantiles, they were open-topped ones in the summer. My sister had to wear a navy gym slip and a white blouse, with a braid girdle, I was not old enough for this, so was sent to a Kindergarten in the town, run by two maiden ladies, and it was called The Ladies School. My first day there was a sunny day, and they put me on a chair in the window in the full sun. I had always had weak eyesight and been allergic to bright light, but this was only discovered when I was fourteen, I was completely dazzled, my eyes streamed with water, and I was most unhappy, but being a very shy child, I was afraid to say anything. I can remember wriggling about on my chair when I wanted to go to the lavatory, as I was afraid to ask, so I wet my knickers. They taught me to tell the time, I was a long time learning the alphabet and however many times they got me to repeat c-a-t, after them, I couldn't see how it could become cat. I can well remember the day when it suddenly dawned upon me.

One day there was great excitement, as my Father had unexpectedly been given leave, when we arrived home from school he was there, we were so happy. He played "Bears" with us and "Father, Father, I've come to confess", and it was just like old times. He was rather worried about the business as trade was slowing down - he hated the Army as he was a business man. As he was on leave he was able to pursue his favourite hobby - which was fishing - he used to go with his friends, and they would hire a taxi, and take their fishing tackle with them. I know my Father always used a large wicker basket to put the fish in, and they would get in the taxi and load it up with bottles of beer and one thing and another, and Mother used to sav "What it cost them for the day out" - they went to Eridge Park, and when they came back, they put the fish out in rows for all their friends to admire. We had a photograph once of my Father - he had pinned the fish on a board so that they could be photographed, they were big fish which looked like plaice or sole. My Mother said he often brought eels home, and when he took them out of the bag, they were still alive, and he used to put them in the sink and he wanted Mother to cook them, and they were jumping about in the sink. Mother said she didn't mind - but when she got older she said "I couldn't possibly do it now, I don't know how I ever did it then!" She said "I either had to boil them, or fry them and they used to jump about in the frying pan." As well as fishing, my Father was very keen on Antiques, and he would go across to the Auction Rooms and buy things. I think Wickendens had the Saleroom at that time, Bracketts took it over later on. He would get all sorts of lovely things and take them back to the shop. That was about all he could do when on leave, as time went so quickly.

When it came time for him to go back, he came into the kitchen (I can remember this) and he kissed us, one by one, we three children - and my Mother, and said to Mother "I'm going away now - and I won't be coming back". Mother wouldn't believe him, and tried to reassure him; how little did we know that it would be the last time we would ever see him.

It was Easter time now, and everything on the Common was beginning to burst into bloom, all the horse chestnut trees were out, some had pink blooms on them and some white, but best of all we liked to see, and smell, the may trees. They were simply beautiful all up Major York's Road, on the left, and the right hand side, but more on the right, and some of them had deep red clusters of flowers, hawthorn, or may trees as we called them. Some were white, but there were one or two pale pink ones which were a cross between the two, and they were beautiful, with a lovely blue sky up above they used to show up, and we loved to walk through the path and to smell the blossom. We liked the gorse when it was out in full bloom, it was very prickly, and we were told that you could make perfume out of it if you picked off a lot of flowers when in full bloom and took them home and poured hot water on them, and steeped them in a tea cup; it didn't smell of anything at all, except water! Sometimes there were marguerites on the Common, but not very many, and the wild daisies when newly out, used to be a lovely deep pink on the underside, we made them into daisy chains. The dandelions were enormous, but we were afraid to pick those - because there was a tale about that if you picked dandelions you would wet the bed! We really believed this, and so did other children.

Grandma used to collect dandelion leaves and make tea out of them, she drank the tea, too. My brother collected butterflies, and it was rather cruel, because when he caught one in a net - he would go home and upstairs, would pin these butterflies on a board, so they had a sort of slow death, and I couldn't bear to see them, as the wings used to flutter, and they got less and less active until they died. He also collected birds eggs - he went bird's nesting, I went with him sometimes, again I didn't approve of this. I remember one day he got hung up in a tree and couldn't get down, and I just stood and laughed at him, and hoped he'd stay up there because I thought he was doing something wrong. He had a lovely collection though, he kept them in a box with cotton wool layers in between, then he would take them out and look at them, one was called a great auk's egg, I don't know where he found some of them, he had an ostrich egg as well, people sold them in shops at one time.

When we were on the Pantiles we were like other people and we would send our blankets to the Beaters on the Common. They collected the carpets as well from houses, because we did not have vacuum cleaners in those days, and there was far more dust about on the roads. The Beaters were strong men who beat the blankets and carpets to get the dust out, and would then clean them as well, it was not unusual to see the blankets strung up on lines between the trees near the Fairground. The dust came out in clouds, as the men beat them with besoms, which were canes plaited, with a handle at the end, and were pliable and strong, as well as light to handle.

Sometimes when we were on the Common we would put our heads right down to the ground and listen to the crickets, they made a strange fluttering sort of sound, and we used to like the dragonflies, they were very pretty, they had lovely opalescent wings, and very long thin bodies, I don't think you ever see any flying about nowadays. There were very tiny blue moth-like butterflies sometimes, near the heather; I haven't seen any for years. We liked picking the wild flowers - there were lots of 'ladies shoes and stockings', they had very short stalks. Then pink and white clover, and white stinging nettles - my sister would always say they wouldn't sting us if they were in flower, and she was right; but other times when they were not in flower we were stung, and our legs were all blistered, the only thing which would help was if we put a dock leaf on our legs, and that cooled them down. We found lots of blackberries in the autumn on the Common, the largest ones were always at the top of the bushes, so we would take a walking stick with us to reach them.

We often went to the rocks near the cricket ground, there were some very high rocks which had sand beneath them on the ground, and I was able to jump off the top of those, and my friends used to stand and watch, as I seemed to be the only one who would jump off them. When we went on the largest rocks we would take a small piece of slate with us and try to carve our initials on the top of the rock, and I spent hours there because it needed so much effort as our hands weren't very strong, as we were small. To try and incise these letters on the rock, every time I went up I made it a bit deeper and then it showed up clearly "J.B." After many years I brought my grandchildren here for a holiday and sent them up to the top of the rocks to find my initials, they could not find them, but I pointed out just where they should be, and at last they cried out "Grandma- we've found them - "J.B." I told them to come down, then gave them the camera and told them to take a snapshot.

Sure enough, there were my initials right where I said they would be, and they will be there for ever, and when they grow up, I hope they will bring their grandchildren to see the initials in years to come.

The Band, Pantiles 1990.

The Pantiles 1914, showing Band far left.

When I was very young there were some bath chairs standing on the Common on Mount Ephraim, waiting for customers, sometimes a donkey would pull one along, but at other times they had open ones which people would sit in, and they were like a large pram with a handle at the back and a hood on top, and a man would push them along so that the old ladies could get some fresh air along Mount Ephraim. Grandma told us about the performing bear which stood on its hind legs and when the Keeper sang a tune the bear would dance in time, it went like this: "Ingy Bingy, Ingy Bingy, Ingy Bingy Bon - Ingy Bingy, Ingy Bingy, Ingy Bingy Bon". The Keeper had a cap laid on the ground for people to put money in, and he always got a lot, and everybody clapped.

When we had a Fair on the Common a firm called Andrews mostly ran it, and the organ music was lovely. It played from perforated paper rolls and could play anything from classical to ragtime, the most popular to start off with being 'I'm Forever Blowing Bubbles', 'The Man Who Broke The Bank At Monte Carlo' and 'At Trinity Church I Met My Doom'. The music was marvellous, and round the front of the organ there were trumpeters and negroes with a miniature band, and they beat various instruments in time to the music, with drums, cymbals and castanets. There were very colourful roundabouts with horses, mostly piebald, with curly brass rods attached to the ceiling, which went through the centre of the horse, so you sat astride, sometimes two on a horse, and the horse glided up and down whilst we hung on to the brass rod, the horses had real hair tails as well as manes, white teeth, and a red tongue, a saddle and stirrups. My Mother used to stand and watch whilst we went round, at first slowly, then at an increasing speed so that we only just caught a glimpse of her as we passed each time.

My sister used to try and win a goldfish in a bowl, she did manage to win one after much trying, but I think we over-fed it, as it only lived two days. My brother liked the rifle range, but I didn't like the bangs when he fired, sometimes if he won they would give him his money back, and then he would spend it all over again. I fancied the Hoop-La, whereby we were given three wooden rings and had to throw them over jars, so that they landed without touching the glass, prizes for this were called Fairings, which were china ornaments made of white glossy china, all different designs with figures of cats or people on them, with the title at the bottom such as "THE LAST IN BED TO PUT OUT THE LIGHT".

There was a tent with a Fat Lady in it, we paid 2d each to see her, and she was the largest, and fattest, lady I have ever seen, then there was a lady with four legs, she could only walk by using her arms as legs, so walked like a dog, and ran about the tent very fast on all fours, her language was unprintable!

We had great fun when we visited the tent where the distorting mirrors were - as we went so fat or thin, tall or short, we used to pull faces at each other and laugh until tears ran down our faces and our sides ached.

The coconut shies were very fascinating - but however much we tried, we could never win - the coconuts seemed to have a habit of rising up and down when they were on top of the posts without coming off, we used to think they were nailed on. I was allowed to throw wooden balls at the post, by standing much nearer behind the chalk lines, as I was so small. My brother and sister had to stand on the grown-ups side of the line, one day my sister came in, and she had been across to the Fair on her own, and proudly displayed a coconut. We were spellbound - and said "How did you get that?" She said "I won it, of course,", but we couldn't think how she had managed to win one, when nobody ever could. The next day she went back on her own again, and brought another one home. When she went the third time, I decided to follow her to find out how she was able to be so clever as to keep winning. To my surprise, I saw her talking to the coconut man, who picked up a coconut which was behind the tent in the large pile of them, and handed her one, and she gave him 3d - she had bought it off him. We didn't think she was clever after that! At night the Fairground looked lovely with all the coloured lights and machines with lamps hanging up over the stalls and the music went on till late at night, long after we were asleep.

We had plenty of room at the Pantiles, it was a large house, and if it was our birthday we would have a party. The day before, our mother used to put our hair in curlers as our hair was not very curly; she used long strips of white rag, dampened it, then dampened the ends of our hair, and wound them round the rag. They were very lumpy to sleep on, but when they were undone next morning, our hair was quite curly! We always wore white hair ribbons made of double satin ribbon, and my brother used to wear a Sailor suit (this was before he went to school). Normally he wore grey flannel shorts, and a grey felt hat with brim. We wore white cotton embroidered dresses with ribbon insertion in pink or blue. At the party we used to play Postman's Knock, Statues, Musical Chairs, Blind Man's Buff and Forfeits. Then we had to recite, my brother was very fond of singing, we all wished he would leave off, and as my Father was named after John Gilpin we had to hear 'John Gilpin's Ride to York' and 'Tit Willow'. I had to recite "Three Little Kittens" but my sister turned awkward and would not do anything! We had marvellous jellies and ice creams and cakes to eat, we ate enormous teas, not like they do today.

We always had a comic every week, and generally at Christmas an Annual, which Mother said kept us quiet all day on Christmas day. My brother took a comic called 'Chips' and the 'Magnet', I think that had Billy Bunter in it, the fat boy who was always eating cream buns - we had

Chatterbox and Playbox, and the Rainbow. Mother liked magazines she had Home Chat, and Mab's Fashions because she was very fashion-minded and Tit Bits, and when my brother was older he had the Children's Newspaper, but we didn't like this, he had the Boys Own Paper. Florence would read to us at bed time sometimes, and she read from Hans Anderson's Fairy Tales, The Water Babies, and Grimms Fairy Tales, and I liked StruwelPeter, because it had a picture of him on the front of the book, and he'd got tremendously long hair, and his hands were down by his sides, and his finger nails reached right down to his feet. Mother took the Daily Mail, and they had a Fancy Dress Competition on the Pantiles, and it said they were going to judge the costumes on the Bandstand, all the children had to dress up in Daily Mails. There was a great demand at the Newsagents for the paper and they sold out very quickly, we made paper hats and dresses out of them, but we did not win a prize, the feature in the paper for children was Teddy Tail, so we all had to show Teddy Tail on some part of our outfit - the children did look funny covered in newspaper clothes!

We had Swimming Baths in the town, both indoor and outdoor - the indoor ones were in Monson Road, I went there when I was about seven, I didn't like water. My Father hated it apparently, he was scared of it, but I must have inherited his fear without realising it, I was standing watching my sister who was having a lesson, I was on the edge of the Pool when a boy came along quietly behind me and suddenly threw me into the water. It went all over me, and I was quite certain I was drowning, I was terrified, and when it came to my turn to have a lesson they said they would have to test my nerve to see whether I was going to be any good or not. They put a pair of reins on me, and drew me backwards and said the water must go over my head. I screamed the place down, and they said "You will never be any good" and I never tried again after that. If I go to the seaside I only paddle!

When we were on the Pantiles the Rag and Bone man used to come round sometimes, we never gave him anything, but could always hear him coming from a distance, as he used to call out "Bone . . . . Bone . . . . Bone . . . ." Any rags which he collected he sold to a factory, and they made them into paper. We had a muffin man as well, he carried a tray on his head with lots of muffins for sale, the muffins were covered with a white cloth to keep the dust away, he also carried a handbell which he used to ring, Sunday was his favourite day for calling, and once or twice we bought some from him, and they were very nice, rather like crumpets. Sometimes we went for a walk up Mount Sion way, through the Grove, past Claremont Road and up the top to Camden Park, and at the very top of the hill on the right hand side, there was a small house, and outside in the garden, there were two ornaments, and they were men - each sitting astride a crocodile, with a bow and arrow. There were two of these crocodiles, I think they were made of wood and they were a greyish white, but green with age, and all their skins had fins sticking out all the way along. These men were very life-like with very straight legs. Their faces and eyes showed up, they were aiming, they had a bow in one hand and an arrow passing through the bow, they were about to fire them. They were quite close together, side by side, and they were there for years and years, we used to like to look at these crocodiles. Recently I walked up that way to see how they looked, as it was some time since I had been up that way - to my surprise, a lady came out from the house, and I said "What ever has happened to the crocodiles?" She replied "They have been vandalised" she said "It's broken my heart, nobody knows where they came from originally, they have been here for years and years, it may be hundreds of years." She said "They came along in the night, nobody heard them, they broke one in half, and the other one was lying on the ground and they are so badly damaged because they were brittle with age, that we think they are beyond repair." It was an absolute shame, they never did things like that years ago.

We had a request from Grandma to try and find a home for some of Blackie's kittens, her cat had a total of 26 kittens over the years, and I think most of the black cats in our town were related to Grandma's cat. She always managed to find a home for the kittens, but sometimes was at her wits end to know what to do with them!

She used to buy ice cream for us when we went to watch the Cricket matches, there were two ice cream salesmen and they had a barrow each, with a round bucket in it which had ice to keep it from thawing, it was beautiful ice cream made with real fruit and cream, one man was called De Mashio, and the other one was De Duca, they were both Italian. One left his cart near the Cricket Ground, and the other one near the Fairground, and they came on different days, they did a roaring trade, especially when Cricket or the Circus were on.

DELIGHTFUL

Motor Char-a-Banc Tours

By permission of the Photochrom Co.

By the Company's Luxurious Mauve Char-a-bancs.

THE MOST ENJOYABLE WAY OF SPENDING YOUR HOLIDAY.

Autocar Services Limited, OPERA HOUSE BUILDINGS, **TUNBRIDGE WELLS**

TELEPHONE **676.**

Hoopers Department Store, 4 Mount Pleasant Road, Tunbridge Wells.

Entrance to High Rocks, Tunbridge Wells.

Tea Time at the Corn Exchange, Pantiles.

Men Weeding the Brighton Lake, Tunbridge Wells.

Chalybeate Springs, the Pantiles, drinking the water.

Fox Brothers of the Pantiles, founded 1892.

The Font, King Charles The Martyr Church, the Pantiles.

Todd's Vintry, the Pantiles, Tunbridge Wells.

CHAPTER SIX

OUR FATHER IS KILLED

The High Rocks - we were going by train from the West Station as a special treat to see the High Rocks. My brother was the eldest, he was put in charge, and we set off to walk along the Eridge Road to the Station as it was not very far. It was very dusty, in fact clouds of dust came up from the road, as a carriage or two went past, and the Dust Cart came along, which was a good thing as it sprinkled water over the road to lay the dust. It had a wide bar across it with perforated holes, so that a small spray of water came out when required. It was a very rusty old car, but very useful, the ladies used to hold their skirts up when it passed as they were afraid of being splashed.

When we got to the Station, the train was drawn up ready to leave, my brother bought three children's tickets to the High Rocks Halt. The train was belching smoke, the men were shovelling coal in near the Driver's seat, and soon there was a great hissing of steam. The railway men were very busy tapping the lines with hammers to make sure the rails were sound, we got in, sat down on the plush seats, and admired the photographs of seaside places which were enclosed in glass panels above the seats (some carriages had a mirror on the wall in the middle, with pictures on either side) but this one didn't. We could draw the blinds down if the sun got in our eyes, there were nets above our heads made of string with round holes in them, so that people could put luggage in them if it was not heavy. We could open the windows by using a wide leather strap with holes which fitted into notches, so that it could be at different heights, you had to give it a tug if it reached the top, to make sure it was shut tight. Just below the window pane, on the door, it had a message in French, and it said "Ne pas se pencher au dehors", we were told that it meant we were not to lean out of the window, but used to wonder if it was in German - as we were at War with the Germans. We were also told that a passenger on the other Station had been leaning out of the window when the train went under the bridge, and he was decapitated! There were brass ashtrays on the wall near the door, and I always wondered how they emptied them, as they were fixed on. When it was time to move off, the Station master blew a whistle and waved a flag, and we were off.

We soon arrived at the High Rocks as it was only a short journey and the train stopped fairly near the entrance. We all three walked along the road, sharing a bag of sweets between us, Edinburgh rock as a special treat. Near the rocks on the right hand side there was a nice round thatched summerhouse. It had a tiny window, an open doorway with a wooden bench to sit on which held three people. It was used when waiting for the carriage and horses to take people to Tunbridge Wells, as a Waggonette with coachmen and horses used to go to and from the West Station, if people didn't wish to go by train, they could wait in the summerhouse. We crossed the road to the High Rocks entrance, went up the steps and paid the man who was in charge a penny to go in. He pressed a lever, so that we could go through the turnstile. We went along a path on the right hand side because we were looking for the Maze, we soon found it. We went round and round, we were the only ones in it, and we kept going back to the beginning, with much laughter; in the end, we found the way out. Then we could hear music further along, there was a Tea dance in progress. There was a flat piece of ground with some round tables and chairs all ready for tea, and a Dance Band on a small platform with ladies and gentlemen dancing round and round. We stood and watched, then noticed movement through the trees, went to investigate and found it was a long swing, consisting of a wide plank of wood suspended from two trees far apart, fixed on with chains. The swing swung to and fro, with about ten people on it all at once, standing up. They started it by two people at each end putting one foot each on the ground, to make it gather speed it went quite fast in the end, in fact children were not allowed to go on it, so we left there and started our climb up the rocks. It was terribly steep, and I kept getting out of breath as it was a job to keep up with the other two. We went higher . . and higher . . and came to a very small bridge as high up in the air as a house, my legs felt all funny when I looked down, I was afraid the bridge might break and we would fall down to the ground. We climbed on and on, crossing several bridges and my brother on one occasion jumped up and down on the bridge to frighten me, but I knew he was only playing. We at last found the way down, and had to look for the Bell Rock, we got a stick each, knocked hard on it, but it didn't sound much like a bell, then there was a rock with a lot of writing on it, the other two could read some of it, but I couldn't. The trees were growing right out of the tops of the Rocks, all their roots were showing, we could see the Railway Line when we were up very high, but took care not to go too near the edge. When we got outside we sat in the summerhouse waiting for the Waggonette, but it didn't come, so we decided to walk, as it was not very far, and it was a nice spring day.

We went over the fields near the railway and saw a beautiful lot of bluebells, wild orchids, and primroses and picked an armful each, we were walking back towards Tea Garden Lane when a lady came along, and saw us with these flowers and said "Wherever did you find those lovely flowers?" We told her, and she said "Would you sell me them?" We had a quick discussion - and agreed between ourselves to accept the offer, and she gave us a shilling! This was a lot of money, even divided into three, so we hurried home, and told Mother what had happened, and she made us put part of it in our money boxes and let us have a little for sweets, we bought some chocolate buttons with hundreds and thousands on them, we did enjoy our outing.

When we were older - my brother had been given a bicycle by my Uncle Harry so, as we hadn't one, my sister and I were sent to Reads Bicycle shop in Goods Station Road to hire one. My sister had a Raleigh, and I had a Rudge Whitworth, we hired them for one day only, I'd never been on a bike, so we all had to walk over the Common towards the High Rocks, and to push them, as it was quiet over there, and then try out the bikes. My sister managed very well - having been on a friend's one before, I was all right until it came to turning a corner, when I always fell off, I think I turned too sharply so that the handle-bars jerked, and threw me to the ground. Undismayed, I tried over and over again, till I mastered it, all was well until I went to get out of bed the next morning, when not only was my bottom black and blue, but I was as stiff as a poker. Never mind, I was given a second-hand bicycle after that, and tenacity of purpose stands one in good stead.

When we got to the High Rocks we decided to have a break, and walked along the top of a high stone wall, which divided the High Rocks Inn garden from the road. They kept pigs, and the pigs were just under the wall inside the garden, we were afraid we would fall down on top of the pigs, but we never did. They had a pond there going down the hill, someone said that there was a person drowned in the pond one day.

The next morning we were having breakfast when the Postman arrived. He gave my Mother a letter, she opened it - and burst into tears. I'd never before seen her cry, I don't think I ever saw her cry after that. I certainly did then, and she said "It's your Father . . ." and we said "What is it?" and she said "He's been killed, He's been killed in the War" and she burst into tears again. It was terrible, it really was . . . My Father was in charge of one of the guns of the Royal Garrison Artillery, this was in 1917, at Ypres. In the battle of Ypres conditions in the trenches were diabolical, they were half full of water, and thick mud, and the fellow who shared one of the trenches with my Father was young, like himself, and had a young family. They both agreed that if one should be killed and not the other, the one left would inform the widowed wife; this he did, and sent my Father's watch strap home as it was all that could be found of him, as he was blown to pieces by a shell. The fellow was the one who sent Mother the letter, she received an official one from the War Office a day or so later.

It was to bring a great change into our lives, because we had the business on the Pantiles which was rented, and Mother couldn't run it with three young children to look after and poor health. She had a Manager to pay - and staff, so we had to sell the contents of the shop as that was all we had, apart from the furniture in the house. Word soon spread along the Pantiles as to what had happened, and all my Father's friends rallied round. I was only four years old but had a birthday the following week, and I can remember some of my Father's friends by name - he had Mr Pelton, Mr Pratley, Mr Wickenden, Mr Fooks, Mr Bishop, Mr Hayward, Mr Frank Hayden, Mr Groves, Mr Clements, Mr Nicholson, Mr Bishop (both Chemists), Lindsay Hermitage and Charles Simpson. They had a meeting to discuss what could be done to help my Mother, and there was a Charitable organisation in the town and they knew all about my family and were very concerned. They really saved the day for us because they applied for the Widow's Pension for Mother from the Government, as he was killed on active service, it was only £3.6s.8d a week on which she had to keep us all, this set amount was never altered or increased from the date of my Father's death until my Mother died at the age of 59 years. It was not enough to feed and clothe us all as well as educate, so this organisation arranged to send my brother to Boarding School in Hertfordshire and to provide the School uniform, and to pay for we two girls to go to a Boarding School a few miles away. This was a real Godsend, and we have all been most grateful for all the marvellous help it gave us. My brother was a credit to the School as he did extremely well thanks to good tuition, plus brains, and we girls had excellent grounding for our futures and put it to good account. Mother was responsible for feeding us in the holidays, and my brother was sent away almost at once to Boarding School, he was nine years old. I think I was eleven when I was sent away, and my sister thirteen. I went as a weekly Boarder to a School at Southborough when I was seven, and then had about two or three years at the County School before going to Boarding School. My sister also went there at the same time, and left when she was seventeen, then took a Secretarial course.

When I was a weekly Boarder I can remember how cold I was in bed, and the food was atrocious, we used to have boiled rice in water with a pat of margarine for pudding, and brawn for the first course, which was a cold jelly, very salty, and when we walked upstairs we could feel it wobbling in our stomachs. We had excellent food at the other School in the country.

Meantime, the business contents and stock went up for sale by Auction, and Wickendens conducted the sale, and with the proceeds, Mother had enough to buy a small house, and kept enough furniture to furnish it. We lived in a flat to begin with, it was a rented one in Queens Road. The following year in 1918 the War finished, and my Father was killed at the end of September 1917, if only he had lived through the War, how different everything would have been. I would probably have married a Tunbridge Wells man and not had to go to live in Scotland and Cornwall, and leave my beloved Tunbridge Wells.

My Father was so ambitious, and was a business man, and he made the supreme sacrifice. He had to give up business and all his future. He was a brilliantly clever man, and if he had lived I don't doubt that he would have had premises about the size of Weekes, or the Army and Navy Stores; because at that age he had done very well, he had taken over all the block of shops, and we were left impoverished. From then until we married we were extremely badly off.

My sister and brother both went out to work and did very well, they both married into titled families. I stopped at home because my Mother's health broke down. I was about fifteen when it happened, and when I left School at an early age, sixteen I think, I looked after her from then on, until I got married in 1938, the year before the second World War broke out.

What Mother used to do, was to take in sewing as she was an expert seamstress. When I went to Boarding School, they all wore uniform. In the summer we had to wear tussore silk dresses trimmed with blue, and straw hats with blue bands on them. In the winter we had different clothes and they were all supplied by Waymarks who were the School Agents, they were quite expensive, and Mother couldn't possibly afford it. She was able to arrange an interview with the Manageress who supplied the uniforms and explained her position, and she allowed Mother to copy the outfits exactly. Nobody ever knew, we were dressed the same as all the other girls. In hindsight, when I was at the County School - Mother had very little money - she made me a winter coat out of one which she had cut down from her own. It was black and looked nice, but I also had my sister's discarded hat, gym slip and her shoes, and my brother's socks. In some way, I don't know how, word travelled round my class that I was in these inherited articles, and all the girls got round me and jeered at me and said 'She's got her Mother's coat on, she's got her sister's hat on' and so on . . . and ended up by saying 'She's even got her brother's socks on'. My humiliation was intense, and the next morning I refused to go to School, but would not tell my Mother why. The Headmistress sent for me, and we all dreaded seeing her as she was regarded as the Supreme being, she tried to get me to tell her why I hadn't turned up, but we were trained never to tell tales, so I got a scolding, and joined the class.

In term time Mother moved out of our house and let it furnished, and went to live in a bed sitting-room and take in sewing, so she could earn enough to provide us with food etc. in the holidays. She had to live in all sorts of places, once she lived in the Lonsdale Mansions Hotel and another time in York Road, and it went on like that, and so she managed to save as much as possible, which enabled her to return home and always be sure of having our home for us to come to in the holidays. We owe a lot to her.

I used to jump off the largest rock.

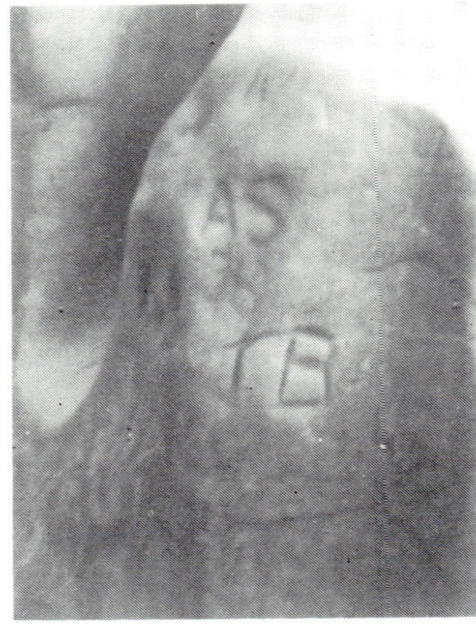

My initials on Harrison rocks.

The High Rocks, Tunbridge Wells.

The War Memorial, Tunbridge Wells.

CHAPTER SEVEN

1918 · WAR MEMORIAL SERVICE

It was 1918 - being the end of the war Tunbridge Wells went en fete, and more or less went mad to celebrate. Mother had gone into what she called Widow's-weeds, they called it deep mourning when everybody went into black from head to foot; black hat, shoes, coat - the lot, and we as Schoolgirls used to wear black arm bands, also black coats; Grandma went into mourning as well. We were taken all round the town to see the decorations which had been put up to celebrate. I remember an arch being built at the top of the Wells hill, where the Cinema is; it was turreted, like a Castle, very well done indeed, with ivy trailing over the top. There was another arch as well, down in Camden Road, but not quite so well done, but much evergreen was used everywhere to make it look nice, and the flags were all out. I don't know how Mother felt when she saw all this, it must have taken a long time to get it all ready, but a long time afterwards when it was ready, they made the War Memorial. As Mother was a young widow, and Father's name was on the Memorial, we were given a front position when it was unveiled because we had lost my Father in the War. All the Town Councillors were there, and the Mayor, and I can remember going, and standing there with my Mother, it made a vivid impression upon me. People sang 'Oh God our help in ages past' and how sad it was; when I think of it now, I feel sad and hope we never have another war.

My Father's brother who lived in Bedfordshire was also killed in the War, and when we visited the Church where he used to go with his parents, we had a look at the pew where the two brothers sat with their Mother, and they had written their initials on the pew 'R.B. and J.G.B.' for Richard and John Gilpin Butcher. How little did my Grandmother realise that one day both her sons would be killed in action. The third son (Uncle Harry) had twin sons, and they were both killed, but not in the War. One was nineteen and one was twenty, so altogether the family lost two brothers, and then twin brothers. Uncle Harry (my Father's brother) started from nothing, the same as my Father, and he went to London and set up in business as an Estate Agent. It was known under his name of Henry Butcher & Co. He was an Auctioneer as well, and he became very well known. His advertisements could be seen in the newspapers as he eventually sold Factories etc, and his premises were in Chancery Lane, the firm changed hands over the years, but still goes under his name, but I think it is now Henry Butcher, Hall and Co. My Father's other brother Fred, did quite well, he went to live at Hastings, he didn't have any children, and he worked at a High Class Gentleman's Outfitters, he later took over the business and extended it, and by doing so became one of Hastings principal shopkeepers. When he retired he was comfortably off, he was endowed with the family brains which were bestowed upon him. Uncle Harry, his other brother who was an Auctioneer and Estate Agent, used to drive around in a Rolls Royce, he had a Chauffeur at the time, and had the Coat of Arms on the side door of the car, our family could be traced back to the twelfth century. He wasn't very old when he died, he was in his sixties, and one morning when his Butler went to call him, he found him dead in bed, he had died in the night.

I will give you a list of names of the shopkeepers who were trading on the Pantiles in 1914-1915 at the end of this chapter. Time passes and we are now at 1921 - we had bad news about Grandma - she came in to see us one day, and she said "I'm not well, I've been to the Doctor", so Mother said "Well, you look well enough", because Grandma always had a good colour. She couldn't bear to be told that she looked well, so Grandma looked at my Mother and she said "That colour is no use to me". She had been to see the Doctor and he confirmed that she had got gall stones - we were surprised because Grandma always carried the potato in her petticoat pocket, and said if she did that, she would never get gall stones. The Doctor said she would have to go to the General Hospital which was in Grosvenor Road, the Catholic Church called St Augustine's was opposite. The Hospital stood well back from the road, it was a very old building. Grandma was duly booked in for the operation, and great apprehension ensued all round, as we were very fond of her, and could not imagine what it would be like without her. Three days after, she was admitted, and was put in the Women's Ward, with cubicles divided by a curtain in between each bed. She chatted to the woman in the next bed to her, and said "What are you in here for?" So the Woman said "Gall stones", so Grandma said "That's funny, so am I". They sympathised with each other, and consoled each other, and the next morning it was time for the lady to go down to the Theatre for the operation, it being her turn to go first as she had been admitted the day before Grandma. She was taken down to the Theatre and the Nurse drew the curtains back and Grandma was left on her own, she dozed for most of the time until bed time. Next morning Grandma looked round and noticed the curtains round the next bed were open and the bed was empty, so she said to the Nurse "Where is the other lady?" The Nurse replied "Oh. she's gone". Grandma said "Well, that was quick, I didn't think you could have it done quite as quickly as that!" "Oh no, she had it done - but she's gone". So Grandma said "Gone where?" The Nurse looked up at the ceiling, and of course Grandma said "Good gracious, you don't mean to tell me she's dead?" Nurse said "I'm afraid so." So Grandma looked at her, she said "Get my clothes, get me my clothes, I'm not stopping here another moment, I'm going home straight away, get me my clothes". So they gave her her clothes and she came out, and knocked on our door, and said "I'm not having any more to do with gall stones, I'm keeping them, even if I've got them. I'm not going back there again, the lady in the next bed to me has died and I'm not going to have the operation - now, or later." She lived to be about seventy-five and merely died of old age, she must have been sixty years old when that Hospital visit happened, and she never mentioned gall stones again, it cured her for good. I can't remember whether she kept the potato in her pocket or not.

I was on my way home one day from the County School, Mother had asked me to buy a piece of music in a shop called Rabson's in Vale Road. I decided to take a short cut through the Station, so leaving Mount Pleasant I went past the gate, along the bridge, then started to go down the stairs. There was a short flight (just as it is now) then a curve with a sort of platform, then a small flight of straight stairs. When I got to the flat platform part I came upon a group of boys aged about 10 - 15 years of age. There were about five of them, they ambushed me, pounced on me, got me down on the ground. I couldn't imagine what on earth they were trying to do, as I was completely innocent at that age and hadn't got a clue as to what was going on. One of them pinched me and got my skirt up, and tried to pull my clothes down, and for some reason or other I must have realised that they didn't mean any good, and I fought them. I lashed about like a mad thing, I kicked, and I punched, and did anything I could think of, to ward them off, and I succeeded in getting away from them. It made a big impression on me, and when I went home I didn't like to tell my Mother, I don't know why. I've always remembered that, and I often think about it when I go down that bridge. I look round behind me, I know it's silly of me at my age to do that, but I suppose it did affect me in a way, because now I'm old, I understand what they were trying to do. I don't know whether they would have stood any chance, but there was nobody about at that particular time, whether one of them was keeping guard, I wouldn't know. It was not a very nice experience, I must have been nine or ten years old at the time.

We used to buy a lot of music at Rabsons, mostly Operatic, as Mother was a born pianist and could play by ear if it was popular music. When we were living in the flat in Queens Road the old lady downstairs had a lot to put up with, as my Sister and I used to tap dance on the floor boards to the music. My Brother was hardly ever at home, so did not have the home life which we had. When my Sister was older she played the piano quite well, but only from the printed sheet. I was expected to take music at School and was not very interested. We had to practise in huts outside, and it was so cold. I passed the Primary examination, and then the Intermediate, but nowadays I cannot play a note, only chop sticks. It seems unbelievable, as when I had a bicycle and stopped riding it, twenty years afterwards I was able to get on one, and ride straight away!

Now I will give you a list of shopkeepers on the Pantiles reproduced from a 1914 list:

Here is London Road, Right Side

	FIRE ALARM
2	Spencer & Son, shirt makers, hosiers and hatters.
2a	Hughes, G.O., dealer in antiques.
2b	The Vulcanizing Company.
4	Boots, cash chemists.
CHALYBEATE SPRINGS	
	Chatfield, Mrs, *Dipper*
	Mercer, Mrs, *Dipper.*
8 & 10	Fox Bros, hosiers etc.
12	Groves, H.G., art gallery.
14	Groves, H.G., sub Post Office, telegraph office and saving bank.
16	Groves, H.G., stationer.

Here is Flat House passage

18	Nicholson, chemist.
18b	Ye Pantiles Curio.
22	Porter, Mrs, wool and toy shop.
24	Tolson's wool shop.
26 & 28	Cadena Café Ltd.
30	Sturt, F.W., optician.
30	Pearl Life Assurance Society.
30a	Harrington, John, Ye Olde Sweet Box.
32	Tunbridge Wells Library and Reading Rooms, Natural History Society Hon.Sec., Davies, D.
34	Edwards, T.G., tobacco blender.
36	Philpot, I., bootmaker.
38	Barclay & Co. Ltd, bankers - Miller, E.J., manager.
40	John Butcher, antiques.
42	Mercer, G., ladies and gentlemen's tailor.
44 & 46	Parker, W.S., & Hammick Ltd, cooks and confectioners.
48	Aubin, Orpha D., costumier and ladies' tailor, Aubin E.
50 52	. . .

Passage

54	Maynards Ltd, confectioners.
56 & 58	Swan Hotel buffet.
60 & 62	Butcher, John, house furnisher.
64 & 66	. . .
68	Pelton, A.J., bookseller, stationer, librarian, printer, etc.
70 & 72	. . .

Here is Eridge Road Left Side

1	Dust & Co. Ltd., silk mercers, drapers and funeral furnishers. Thomson, R., managing director - London House.
3	Carter, Edward Jas., & Banks, house and estate agents, auctioneers.
5	Fooks, H.W., tailor.
7	Durrant, Edward, grocer and wine and spirit merchant.
9	Ashby, R.A., butcher.
11	Collings, W.E., bootmaker.
11	Women's Social & Political Union

Eridge Road Left Side *(continued)*

13 Biggs, W.E., grocer and wine merchant.
15 King, E., fruiterer.
17 Baker, Herbert F.
Duke of York.
Tolson & Co., poulterers, fishmongers and ice merchants.
21 Johnston, Mrs.
23 Brooman's dining rooms.
25 McCowen & Douglas *and at 79 High Street.*
29 Tompkins & Stevens, cabinet makers.
31 Pantiles Assembly Rooms.
31 Wheeler, E., hairdresser.
31 Figgett, J.
33 . . .
35 & 37 Charlton, John, seedsman and florist.
35 Dodds, Thomas H.
39 & 41 . . .
43 Public Lavatory for Men.
45 Leaver, G.H.
47 Vigor, R.J.
The Corn Exchange
Depot of the West Kent Q.O. Imperial Yeomanry, C. Squadron.
49 Hollis W.
51 Laflin, B.
51 Harris, W.G., & Co. Ltd, Victoria Pantechnicon.
Sussex Assembly Rooms.
57 Coleman, Miss A.M. - Glen Albion.
59 Salmon, Miss.
61 Robinson, Miss - Sussex House.
61 Thompson, Miss.

Here is Linden Park

63 Chapman, Mrs - Maitland House.
65 Hollamby, Miss - Neville Lodge
The Pump Room - Fry G., steward.
Holmesdale Masonic Lodge and Chapter. Pantiles Masonic Lodge.

Pantiles, The Back

70 . . .
68 Pelton, A.J., librarian.
68 Barnes, Miss J., ladies school.
64 & 66 . . .
60 & 62 Butcher, John, carpet warehouse.
Swan Hotel - Schultz, W. Spencer.

Passage

50 & 52 Hall & Co., automobile engineers.
46 Edwards, Mrs J.H.,
Hand and Sceptre Hotel.
44 Parker, W.S., & Hammick Ltd.
42 Mercer, G., tailor etc.
40 Booty, James, undertaker.
38 Miller, E.J.
30 Sturt, F.W., optician.
26 Cadena Café Ltd, The Cadena.
24 Anderson, Miss.
26 Pearless & Sons, solicitors.
22 Porter, Mrs, wool and toy shop.
20 Ellis, Mrs.
18a Hodgkinson, Miss - Flat House.
18 Nicholson, chemist.

CHAPTER EIGHT

COURIER OFFICE FIRE · MOTOR BIKE ACCIDENT

We were coming home from the County School one afternoon when we heard that there had been a fire at the Courier Office in Grove Hill Road. Of course, children always hope they might see what they would call a 'proper fire' one of these days, so we hastened down the town as fast as our legs would carry us. We heard the fire bells going from the Fire Engines, we rushed up Grove Hill Road and the smoke . . . you could see it as we came down the Wells hill, it was belching out above all the buildings, higher than Weekes, right up into the sky, and crowds were gathering. As we came up the hill some of the slates were falling down into the road, and the flames were blazing out of the top of the roof, I have never seen anything like it, it was what you would call a real fire. We were kept back by the Firemen, and had to stand across the other side of the road, but it got such a hold, they couldn't do anything about it, it just burnt and burnt. The bits of timber fell down, I shall always remember it, because I had never seen a fire before, and I don't think I have ever seen one since. I've seen slight fires when people have had a fire caused by a gas mains and it has been extinguished almost at once: this fire gutted the whole building, it was absolutely in ruins afterwards, and the smell of all the burning was awful. It had to be re-built sometime afterwards, I suppose the Insurance Company must have paid out well for it. All the same, they lost trade and they had to have a notice pinned up on the Great Hall Building windows to try and give any news that was going on in the town because they couldn't publish a newspaper for some time.

There were two small shops in Grove Hill Road, as well, but I think they were all right, one was Mr Walton the picture frame maker, and the other one was a man called a Taxidermist, he used to stuff animals. You'd see all sorts of things in the window such as squirrels and owls. He used to skin them and stretch them out on boards, sometimes we saw some and they were half done, and they looked awful in the window. We shuddered, but we were usually fascinated, as we used to wonder what we would see next when we walked past.

Then coming down the hill to go to the High Street we passed Godkins, and they often had a sale on. You could get two items for the price of one, it was called the Rexall chemist, all the things on sale were the Rexall make. Whether we liked it or not, we had to have them to get the benefit of the Two for One offer. Mr Godkin was a tall thin gentleman and he had children, I think two boys and a girl. The sons were named Laurie and Geoff, I cannot remember the girl's name but she was a pretty girl. Near

Godkins was a marvellous shop, it was run by John Brown's Dairy at one time. I know he married twice and they had children, Mr Brown was short, his second wife was very tall - the children were short and tall and very intelligent. They were superb Bakers and the cakes were simply delicious, so fresh, I believe they had a Café upstairs as well, which had a glazed enclosure looking like a miniature Crystal Palace. We went there to a party once at Christmas. Then we had the Scotch Wool Shop, that was really fascinating as they had round baskets on the counter with lots of lovely coloured balls of wool; small round ones, which were only one penny each, we could have any colour we wanted. I used to buy balls to make golliwogs as I was no good at knitting, but was able to make those. Then we came to a Pub called The Hole in the Wall, very small, and some said they sold wines from the rear of the shop. Next, John Allens Shoe Shop, and Christ Church that was built in 1841. It was a very old church, I think we went to Sunday School there once, I know we went to a Church party, and I was dressed as a Christmas Fairy, I still have the photograph. Then we had Farrers the Jewellers and Goldsmiths, it was a lovely shop with an island window like an arcade. Next came the Intemational, a very large Grocers, which seemed to sell everything. It was next to Bracketts, and after that came Irish the Drapers, they had a son Freddie. There was Hawards the Ironmonger who was a friend of my Father, and then there was a first class shop opposite Castle Street, called Stacey Marks, an Art shop, one of our favourites. They had beautiful pictures, and there was an Art Gallery upstairs. Mother was very keen on one picture called The Sampler, I used to like the ones of children by Mable Lucie Attwell.

There was Frank Hayden, the Ironmonger and Alan Parsons the Coal Office -I think I have left out Lindsay Hermitage - I apologise if the order is wrong, but please make allowance for my childhood memories. We bought our piano from Hermitages, it was a Spencer upright Grand, and they used to come and tune it. On the other side of the road, starting opposite Godkins, was Breeds, the Cutlers. They sold an enormous assortment of scissors and cutlery, it wasn't a very big shop, but it had such a large stock, they would sharpen things for you. Mr Holman was the man who ran it and he was very keen on Oxfam, he used to collect stuff for them and put it down in the cellar, and then send it off to Oxfam. There were three piano shops, Elliott & Starmers, Murdochs, and L.P. Barnes, one of them could have been taken over by the other - I'm not sure about that. Then the pipe shop, Mr Ascough ran it. In a corner, chained to the wall, he had a full-size walking stick, longer than usual, with a man's head (carved) on top. It was the head of an old man, very lifelike, and was there until quite recently. We then had Wickendens Auction offices, they were later on taken over by Bracketts, and next a super shop, Checkermains, known as the Armenian Bazaar, it had lots of Japanese things for sale and it had a fantastic display of oriental things. The Chinese dolls were lovely in their satin kimonos with very white faces and black hair and shoes. They sold sticks of scented sandalwood, and paper flowers, which when put into a cup of water would swell and open into flowers like waterlilies, we used to be very fond of those. I used to spend hours looking in there, and she didn't mind how long we were, she had a very handsome son, who was about the first fellow to have a motor bike in Tunbridge Wells. May's the Needlework shop was on the corner of the High Street, and across the road was Seymour Cousins the Photographers; Mother worked there before she married my Father.

Some years later on, there was a shop on the corner of Chapel Place, on the right, named Sanders the Biscuit Shop. They had a special offer the day they opened and their window's were totally crammed full of biscuits of every type and kind; they could be bought at 3d or 6d a pound, in tins, in packets, in jars, an amazing display. The biscuits were sold by weight and taken out of the containers and packed into brown paper bags. When the shop opened, half the town turned up, as considering you could have any kind of biscuits for 6d maximum a pound, they were remarkably cheap. We had to queue outside, and people were coming away with five or six pounds of biscuits, we went back two or three times as we liked biscuits.

Coming down Chapel Place there was Halls Bookshop run by Mr Pratley. He had a wooden box outside with cheap books at ld each. Then, King Charles the Martyr's Church where I and my brother and sister were Christened in that lovely Font. We never went up into the Gallery, Queen Victoria used to sit up there when she went to Church, but we always sat downstairs. And then we had to wend our way home, as we were no longer living on the Pantiles, but were at St Johns Road, we rented a flat in Queens Road.

Every day, Mother used to let us have a bar of chocolate, it was Fry's chocolate cream, that was my favourite, about 2d for a bar, and there was a shop opposite, on the main St John's Road - a grocers shop which sold chocolate. His name was Mr Lane, and I was sent each afternoon to buy a bar of Fry's chocolate cream for myself, and a whipped cream walnut for Mother. One day she gave me the money, and I was so keen to cross the road quickly, that I came down the steps from our flat to cross the road to reach the main road, and there was a motor bike coming along. It wasn't going very fast, but I thought I could get there before the motor bike, but I misjudged my distance, and the next thing I knew, I was down on the ground, he had knocked me over. The crowd gathered very quickly, but I have never seen anything like the man's face . . . his face, I can see it today, it was as white as paper. He was a fairly young fellow, and he hadn't a hat on, I could tell you what he was like to look at after all this time, as it so shocked me to see his face looking so pale, obviously because I was a child - and he had knocked me down - and he did not know what damage he might have done. I can remember as I was knocked down, rolling to and fro in the gutter, I suppose it was with the vibration, and people came along and lifted me up and one of them said "I know where she lives, she lives in that house over there". I hadn't got the chocolate cream and it was through being so eager that made me misjudge my distance. My Mother came out, and I was taken into the house, and I wasn't too bad at all. In spite of this, she insisted upon me going to bed with curtains drawn, I had to stay in the dark all afternoon, I couldn't imagine why, but I did feel sorry for that man.

We did most of our shopping at St John's as we were living there. A branch of the Nevill Bakery was there, then Gallops the Chemist - Mr Gallop was a very serious sort of man and he was rather bald, he had very little hair. It used to interest me because he used to brush it across his bald head and having a few strands of black hair he tried to make them go as far across as possible! He had a daughter who went to School with me and one day when I went to buy something he said "You know, my daughter knows you - she comes home and tells us all the stories which you make up, because you love telling stories about different things and the girls can choose anything they like, and you make a tale around it, so she recounts them to us, and we always enjoy them." Then there was Dawes the Ironmonger; Mr Dawes was a very nice man indeed, he had a son who worked in Richardson and Duttson as it was called then, it was the Estate Agents in the Great Hall, it later became Richardson and Pierce. Mr Lane the Grocer whose chocolate we used to buy, had a ginger cat which used to sit in the window. Whenever we went in there he would draw out a chair and say "What can I get you ma'am?" He kept a jar of sweets on the counter and he always used to pass one to me, I knew he was going to offer me one when we went in there, we regarded him as a friend. Then there was Littletons the Drapers, a rather old - fashioned shop, but it sold all sorts of things and was good value for money, there was Lines the Furniture Shop.

Further along we had Cavies - the Greengrocers, old Mrs Cavie was helped by her daughter who served in the shop as well. Mrs Cavie was fat and jolly, the most pleasant woman imaginable. We had rabbits at the time, and she used to cut off all the outer leaves of the cabbages and give them to us for nothing so we could take them home as the rabbits were always hungry, and used to get through mountains of green stuff. They were a pleasant family altogether, it was really a treat to go in and buy something. Next, the Down Lane Chapel, and then there was Skinners School across the road - we were near Beltring Road now, - where they had a Recreation

Ground. They had a Giant - Stride whereby there were chains hung onto a post with a wooden handle across, wide enough to take both hands and we would hang on, and swing out and go round in circles, we liked that, and they had lots of oak trees and we used to collect the acorns from them and feed the pigs in Speldhurst Road. They had a Bowling Green there, and when we got older we played tennis on the hard Courts, my sister and I, and we often made up a foursome with two brothers named Bassett who lived in Beltring Road, we played quite well together. Miss Nunn ran the St Johns Post Office, a very capable woman, and Gilletts the Builders were further along.

We now leave that part of the town and go as far as Mount Ephraim, there was Hillarys; they were a nice family - one son ran a Dance Band called the Melodians, and was very musical. Going down Grosvenor Road, they had W.G. Harris the Furnishers, the General Hospital, and St Augustines Church, Apps the Greengrocers were there. In Goods Station Road we had Reads bicycle shop, they had two attractive daughters; and then there was Stevens the Watchmaker and Horologist, he was a very nice, upright old man, quite strict, and very religious as well. He was really expert, he had two sons and one is still in business. The Father was a very devout man, and the family were so honest they were an example to us all. Going to Church Road, we used to go to Romary's Shop because they sold Tunbridge Wells water biscuits, which were very thin and creamy white and had a slightly salty taste but were delicious. They exported them and sometimes had broken or imperfect ones for sale at a lower price than the perfect ones, and we used to buy them. They had a Factory down town near Eridge Road. On the common was Mount Edgcumbe Hotel which was owned by the Raiswells, their cousins had a Grocers in Tunbridge Wells, at Mount Pleasant.

The Pump Room.

My Father's Grave, Ypres.

CHAPTER NINE

GREAT HALL · SUICIDE

We set out for a walk up the town, my Mother, sister and I. We had bought some lovely cakes from Semadenis' in the High Street, they were Swiss Bakers and used much cream in their cakes; their pastry was marvellous, it was so light. Mother had her hair trimmed at Maison Arthur, whilst we chose the cakes, and then we waited at the Hairdressers for her. Walking past Weekes (this part was Broadway) we came to Maynards and bought some whipped cream bon-bons, these were toffees dipped in icing sugar, Mother had a bar of chocolate Turkish Delight. We looked in the window of the Photographers Gilbert Bowley, called in to see Mr Bishop the Chemist - and he said how tired Mother looked, and that she looked as if she needed to go to bed for a good rest. We then came to the Great Hall, it was a Cinema in 1920 and we used to go there sometimes, but we often went when the talking pictures came. One of the first pictures was "The Broadway Melody", we thought it was wonderful, they had an Orchestra, the lady pianist was always dressed in black, she played the piano and I think it was her husband (who was also in black), he played the violin, the seats were of dark grey velvet with a pattern on them, we saw lots of films there over a period of time - including "Ben Hur", "Frankenstein" (we were afraid to go to bed that night), "Dr Jekyll and Mr Hyde" and lots of Actors and Actresses such as Constance Bennett, Paul Lucas, Betty Davis (we played hockey once with her at Boarding School as she went to a School in the next village), Douglas Fairbanks, John Barrymore and Dorothy Wilding, to name just a few. Then we came to Raiswells the Grocer and Wine Merchant, the son Norman was in the shop, and Hobbs the Chemists and Wickhams the Drapers, he sold children's clothes - I can remember my Mother buying my sister and I a lovely silk cardigan each in a crushed strawberry pink, the shop had an island window, like an arcade, the Tudor Café was higher up, downstairs they sold cakes and pastries, wedding cakes, etc, and upstairs they had a glazed verandah, and we sat there in little wicker chairs and wicker glass-topped tables, it was very sunny and too hot in the summer, they had two other rooms which led into each other, so in the summer we used to sit there instead. Sometimes they played the piano, but I don't remember there being an Orchestra there, like the Cadena Café on the Pantiles.

We crossed the road over to the Ritz Cinema, they had just installed a new organ there and the lady who played it, rose up slowly with the organ from the floor, she waved to everybody when it was coming up, and waved to everybody when it was going down again. It had coloured lights on each side and above the keyboard, and she played catchy tunes on it, it was called a Wurlitzer organ. Coming down the hill - (there were no shops on that side) - we passed the Dentist, Mr Carless, he was called an English and American Dentist I don't know why. Mother said I ought to have a tooth taken out but I wouldn't hear of it as I was scared stiff at the prospect, in those days it was a very painful operation.The houses on that side had long gardens in front of them, so that they stood well back from the road - some people like solicitors were there. Mother used to mention Sir Robert Vaughan Gower, he was a J.P. At the end of the houses was a Hotel called the Lonsdale Mansions, on the corner of Lonsdale Gardens, and up from there, they had the Lonsdale Nursing Home; when I was twenty one I had my tonsils removed in there.

Near the foot of the hill there were two or three shops - Kendalls Umbrellas, (they always used to repair ours if they went wrong in any way) Scholls Foot Shop - I believe Mr Godkin's son opened that, then Dilnott Stokes the Estate Agent. Mother used to go to him, and his son acted as Negotiator when selling property. One day he called at our house as it was for sale; Mother was ill in bed, so I saw him. He had been trying to get the prospective buyer to go up in price, and he came to give the answer, and he said "She is adamant, and will not alter". I had never heard the word 'adamant' before, and I had to go and ask Mother and she explained, we gave in, reduced the price of the house and sold it!

That afternoon I went up town again shopping with my sister, up the Wells hill, we saw a crowd of people. The Police and Ambulance arrived. We asked somebody what had happened - they said "A man in one of the shops has shot himself". We waited - and soon afterwards the Ambulance men came out with a stretcher with a body on it, covered with a cloth. Where the head should have been there was nothing - only a small bump, it looked so strange and someone said it was because he had shot himself in the head - poor man! It was a pity we saw the stretcher as I, for one, have never forgotten it. It came on to rain - and the brick pavements looked lovely when they had been washed by the rain. The bricks were made by the High Brooms Brick and Tile Company, they had a factory at High Brooms, and supplied bricks to other towns. When we got home we told Mother of what we had seen - and she said "Poor man." She had heard that he had money problems as the business was not doing at all well and he could not pay his bills, so that was why he shot himself, we were so shocked to hear it.

Mother sent us to John Brown's Dairy to get some cream for tea, I always loved cream - it was delicious, it was so lovely and thick. They were very good Dairymen, and every Christmas Day, when we opened the front door - there was a pot of cream on the doorstep. It was in a cardboard carton,

Royal
Tunbridge Wells
Art Gallery - -

THE PANTILES
(OPPOSITE THE BAND STAND)

Exhibiting Works
BY THE LATE
CHAS. E. BUTLER
including his famous Masterpiece—

"KING OF KINGS"

ALSO A COLLECTION OF OLD MASTERS

ADMISSION FREE.

Waymarks

THE PLACE FOR VALUE.

Kent & Sussex Courier

12 PAGES! 96 LONG COLUMNS!!
Town, Country & Tonbridge Editions EVERY FRIDAY.

THE
LARGEST CIRCULATION
GUARANTEED

Unrivalled medium for "Wanted" advertisements of all kinds, which are inserted in the following
SIX DISTINCT NEWSPAPERS:—

THE KENT & SUSSEX COURIER, EASTBOURNE GAZETTE,
TONBRIDGE GAZETTE, BRIGHTON ADVERTISER.
TUNBRIDGE WELLS GAZETTE SUSSEX COUNTY HERALD,

and appear before at least

150,000 Readers.

SCALE OF CHARGES:

Words	1	3	6	13
	s. d.	s. d.	s. d.	s. d.
20	1 0	[illegible] 6	[illegible] 6	10 0
30	1 6	[illegible] 6	6 6	12 6
40	2 0	[illegible] 0	9 0	17 0

(Number of Insertions)

Tunbridge Wells Gazette and Fashionable Visitor. Every Wednesday Morning, One Half-penny.

HEAD OFFICE: Grove Hill Road, Tunbridge Wells. Tel. 1040 (2 lines).
BRANCH OFFICE: 2, Medway Wharf, Tonbridge. Tel. 200

Telephones 370, 866 and 174.

FINEST DAIRY PRODUCE

Supplied to all parts of the Town from Local Dairy Farms.

RAMSLYE FARM,
ERIDGE ROAD,

SPRATTS BROOK FARM,
ERIDGE ROAD.

JOHN BROWN'S DAIRIES

34, HIGH ST.,
30, MT. EPHRAIM
and
19, VALE ROAD;
and
Model Working Dairies:
57, ST. JOHN'S ROAD
and **23, MOUNT SION.**

and on the lid, it had a wreath of holly just printed on, and it said "Merry Christmas". We knew this would be there and then sometimes they would bring it round in a tiny can with a hinged brass lid on it, and put cream in. They made their own butter, and had their own hens eggs as they had a Farm down in Claremont Road, it was developed when I got married and went to Scotland, and became the Farncombe Estate, with a lot of nice private houses on it, and even a School for the children, called Claremont School.

We bought a house in Claremont Road, I was thirteen years old then, and all my spare time in the holidays was spent over at the Farm, looking at the horses and chickens. They delivered by horse and cart, and had about eight horses lined up altogether in the Stables. The delivery men all used to sit down and have a cup of tea when it was the middle of the morning, they had a nice fire going, to keep them warm. I was madly keen on chickens - they kept chickens as well, as that's where all their eggs came from for the customers. I used to go down to the fields and watch these birds, and simply loved the way they used to scratch about in the ground looking for food, and that sort of thing, lovely feathers, and having dust baths, they were very nice indeed. I longed to have a Poultry Farm when I grew up, because I loved the country, that was from being at Boarding School, as we were in a country village, and I always hoped when I grew up I'd marry a Farmer. We had a Farmers Club on the Pantiles, and they met there on a Friday afternoon, sometimes they met in the Pump Room, but mostly gathered at the far end of the Pantiles (not Binns end, the other end). When I was older and in my teens, I used to go along there and stand about, hoping that one of them might ask me to marry him - they were young farmers, very smart looking, and some wore fawn breeches and leather boots or leggings, tweed jackets and yellow waistcoats, or check ones. I don't think they even noticed me, as I was only a teenager, and certainly did not guess what I had in mind! All my life I wished I could have married a Farmer, I would have loved it, people say it is hard work, but it would not have bothered me, because I would have liked being with all the animals and looking after them, making the butter and cream and collecting the eggs.

Talking about milk and Farms - we did not have any refrigerators in those days so when it was hot in the summer, we always had to boil the milk, generally before we went to bed, so that it would keep overnight. It used to form a thick skin on the top, it was the cream, I loved that, and had it on my Grape Nuts as my sister didn't like it. The milk was delivered, often in a jug (which we held out, and the milkman filled) otherwise it was in a can. We had a terra cotta flower pot affair which was rather like a tiny chimney pot, and covered the milk over with this to keep it cool, being careful to immerse the pot in cold water first as it was porous material, so retained the moisture. When we wanted to use the milk we would put it into a small jug, and then cover it with a muslin net cover which had beads all round it to weight it down, so that the flies could not get at the milk!

In the summer we had a Concert Party which played in the Grove, Ballard Brown was the man who was in charge. I must have been about fourteen or fifteen then, we used to really enjoy going to the performances which were twice a day. They had good amateur actors and actresses, who had to be pretty versatile, as they were expected to be able to sing and dance and be good actors. Their costumes were not very elaborate, but they put on a good performance, all the same. One afternoon they gave the children the chance to enter a competition for local talent, I entered it, but did not realise what an ordeal it would be to go up on to the stage and face the audience. I chose to sing "Alice Blue Gown" but instead of facing the audience, I was so shy that I held my head down and my voice did not carry. I tried "You are my honeysuckle" but that was not any better, and I didn't win a prize, but we really used to enjoy it. It was very well attended, it was very fine entertainment, I can't ever remember us having to pay. We used to stand up and listen, there were not many seats, if any. I enjoyed it so much, that it made me think I would like to go on the Stage when I was old enough, as a career.

I remember my Mother wanted to make me go to the Dentist (because she realised that my teeth did need to be extracted) - I walked up and down Mount Pleasant hill with her and refused to go in. When the time came, we argued and argued, and as we had an appointment Mother used every kind of persuasion that she could think of to induce me to go in. In the end, the only way she persuaded me was, that she said that if I went in to have it done, I could go on the Stage when I grew up, and she won; but I never went on the Stage!

About this time I developed a hernia, and the Doctor said he thought I would be better to have it done before I had to leave home, as I was about to go to Boarding School; so he booked me in at the General Hospital, it was in the School holidays, and wherever I went with Mother and we met our friends Mother used to tell them about it. They all used to look at her, and then look at me and say "Aren't you lucky, you'll have a lovely time, with lots of other children". Of course, that was persuading me to go - I went off, and thought I was going on holiday. When the time came and I was in there, I wondered why they wouldn't let me have anything to eat at breakfast time, and then a Porter came along and he had a red blanket, and wrapped that round me and said "I'm going to carry you downstairs to the Theatre". I thought I was going to see a Play or Concert Party - when we got down there he took me into the operating theatre (you may find this unbelievable, but it is true) and they laid me on this stretcher type of bed.

I had got a white gown on, and they came over and they put a mask over my nose, and they poured some liquid on it, which of course was chloroform. When they did that I did not like it, I shook myself, so that it fell off. The chloroform didn't go on the gauze. At that moment a door opened opposite me and a man came out (it was the Doctor) all dressed in white trousers and he had a mask on, and he looked horrific - that really scared me. Then it dawned on me that something funny was going on, so I decided I would put up a fight, and they had to hold me down, and I fought like a tigress, I really did, and then I remember them pouring some more of that stuff on, and the next thing was, I had gone off to sleep, and I was chloroformed! When I came round, I felt this terrible pain in my stomach, and I could hardly breathe because I was very tightly bandaged, the pain . . . was intense . . . however, I was in the children's ward with others, and like all children - I was very resilient, and after two or three days I wasn't too bad.

When mother came to see me, she brought me a bar of Fry's chocolate cream, as she knew I liked that. We were not allowed to have sweets in there, so I hid it. I pushed it down between the bandages on my stomach, so that the Nurses wouldn't see it, because they were due to come round. After Mother had left they came round, and of course the chocolate had melted, and I was covered in it. I got into awful trouble with them, so I was unable to have any more sweets after that.

My Godmother from Bedford used to write to me, she sent me a picture postcard every day, when I was there. It was always about cats, as she knew I was very fond of cats. They were doing all sorts of things on the card, some were in prams, some climbing ladders, I saved all of these up, they were lovely, they were really colourful, and I took them all home with me. I have always remembered what it said on one particular one, it said 'The hand that rocks the cradle - rules the roost'. The picture showed a Mother and Father cat with some baby ones in a cradle, and the Mother was rocking the cradle; I had no idea what they meant, when they said that, until I was older, and then I understood. When the Nurses were out of the ward, and they didn't know, we used to jump up and down, but I had still got all the stitches in - it was bad . . . nobody knew. I was only kept in there a short time, and when I came out they said I wasn't to walk anywhere for about a week.

They provided me with a wicker bath chair - it was something like an armchair with one wheel in front, and two at the back. It had a swivel rod attached to the front for steering, on an iron bar, with a wooden handle. It could turn, so that it guided the front wheel and could control it. My brother was home on School holidays, and said he would take me out in this, as I couldn't walk. He took me right across the Common, the little devil used to get me to the top of the hill, and start running down the hill with me, and scare the daylight out of me, because he ran really fast, you know what boys are like! Well, I was all right, and recovered and went back to School. It was a remarkable thing, that quite recently I was in an Antique shop at St John's. The Builders had just demolished the old Hospital, they took part of it down to begin with, because it comprised two buildings. They had a corridor which led through from the modern part to the old part, so they built shops all along where the old part had been, but the new part was a wallpaper shop until it was taken down to make way for a new multi-storey car park. They must have found the bath chair in the Hospital before the demolition men went in. When I went into the back part of the Antique shop, lo and behold, there was the bath chair, I couldn't believe my eyes! I would have liked to have bought it, but couldn't think of anywhere I could keep it. It was not the sort of thing you could offer to a visitor to sit on! When I had thought it over, I went back the second time, and they had sold it.

They used to have a market in Calverley Road every Saturday, they were only allowed to be there from one o'clock I think, and when it was time all the men with barrows used to be waiting round side streets and a bell used to ring directly it was one o'clock and the men used to run at top speed to see whether they could get their 'Pitch', as they liked to be in the same place every week. The barrows were outside the shops in the road, some on each side, and they sold fish and vegetables and firewood - bundles of chopped sticks called pimps, 7 for 6d, tied round the middle with a piece of wire. They sold pretty well everything, unskinned rabbits which were hanging up. We hardly ever went, we were not allowed, but we used to be amused when we saw the men running along with the barrows. They were there for years and seemed to do a good trade.

In 1922 we had the Great Storm. I was at the County School at the time, and so was my sister; she was in a different class as she was two years older, I was ten. The sky got very dark early one morning - it got more and more dark as time went on, it took the whole day to arrive. By the afternoon when I was due out of School, it was so dark, it was almost like the middle of the night, this would be soon after three o'clock. The blackness spread from Tonbridge over the whole town, it was most frightening to see, I had never seen anything so dark in the day time. I was waiting for a bus by St John's Post Office and all of a sudden something came out of the sky, and I couldn't think what it was. I picked it up, and there were hailstones, without any exaggeration, the size of tennis balls; I'd never seen anything like it in my life. Then all of a sudden, there was a dreadful flash of lightning and the storm began. The heavens opened . . . the lightning was red, and blue and green and all colours, and the thunder was indescribable, and all these things falling out of the sky - I didn't know what to do. The bus hadn't come and nearby there was a Garage which sold Morgan cars and a school friend lived over the shop with her parents, they looked out and saw me standing there, and they called me to go into their house to take shelter - well, I was petrified, and I used to like storms before that, but unfortunately, the Mother sat me on her lap in the middle of the bay window which looked out right on to the street with a three dimensional view! As we were upstairs we could see in every direction, and I screamed, and screamed, I can't tell you what it was like, it was all Hell let loose, and of course the more the lightning flashed, the more it frightened me. The Mother used to jog me up and down on her lap to comfort me, but of course she still kept me in the window - if she had put me somewhere away from it, or let me hide up, it would have been so much better, and because of that I developed an awful fear of thunderstorms and I've had it ever since, which isn't surprising, because I was away from home, was away from my Mother, away from any friends or anyone who knew us, in a total stranger's house with a stranger I had never seen before, and I was only ten, no wonder I was scared, my sister was all right, because she stayed in the Schoolroom with all the other girls as a group, and they had the lights on, and the blinds drawn. It went on for hours, we thought it would never finish, I had to go home - and get down to Claremont Road in some way, I was unable to go down the town, as it had been so flooded, and the hailstones were so big, that they blocked up all the gutters and the men had to use poles to try and clear the drains. We couldn't go down to Weekes as they were flooded, the water went down into their basement and spoilt all the stock, and so I had to go all round the side streets, I ended up somewhere near Cumberland Walk, to get up to Claremont Road, and up Mount Sion. But the windows . . . Wherever you went they were cracked or broken, branches of trees had been torn off, and were scattered all over the ground, and whenever Ascension Day comes round each year, I'm always worried, as that was the day it happened, and as to whether we would have another storm on that particular day, I hope I never live to see another one like it, I think I would die of fright if so, because they did have another storm about ten or twenty years later, and they thought just because the hailstones were the size of golf balls - they said they had never seen anything like it, they didn't know what they were talking about, as if they had been alive when that one was on, it was about ten times worse, it was awful, Weekes had to sell up all their stock from the basement because it was all flood damaged.

When I got home, (and on the way had to pick my way past all the trees and things), Mother was jolly glad to see me, she thought I was in School all the time, it was just as well she did not know what I was going through. My sister grew up with a fear of thunderstorms just the same as me because of it, I tried to cure myself, and still do now, but of course Tunbridge Wells does get bad storms, the trouble is that it is hilly here, the storms go round and round, and then they go quiet; only to join up with a rumble and start all over again. I don't mind so much in night time as I can cover my head over in bed, but in the day time I don't like it, I go and sit on the stairs. I certainly couldn't go out-doors, we used to have women bus conductresses years ago, it would never have done for me to be one, as I would not have been able to be out in it. So that was the Great Storm, as they called it. They had photographs in the Courier about it, and there was one showing my sister standing at the bottom of the Wells hill in her gym frock, watching the men with poles who were trying to clear the drains of hailstones. My goodness me, I never want to see a storm like that again.

The Ideal Rendezvous for

LUNCHEONS &
DAINTY TEAS

CHAPTER TEN

CUSTOMS · FASHIONS · TRADE · TOWN RESIDENTS

Some tradesmen in Mount Pleasant and Calverley Road - Woolworths - I well remember the day they opened Woolworths, it was like Aladdin's Cave. It was in Calverley Road, and the shop was called the threepenny and sixpenny Stores. It was crammed full of items, nothing over sixpence, long strings of pearls (very good wax-filled reproduction), buckets, brooms, clothes horses, basins, saucepans, china, glass, and everything under the sun. People who spent five shillings were able to have the goods delivered, and a friend who was getting married who spent ten shillings more or less completely equipped her kitchen, including cutlery, glass and china etc.

At this time there was a war on between the Redcar and Autocar Bus Companies, it was possible to go all the way from Tunbridge Wells to Tonbridge for 1d. Redcars were red or mauve I believe, and the Manager of the Autocar was Mr Oscar Pritchard. Sampsons the Antique Dealers had a shop opposite the Autocar premises. It was enclosed by railings where there had once been a garden, they had stone statues outside for sale. The National and Provincial bank on the next corner had a branch of the Junior Imperial League upstairs,the Young Conservatives held meetings and Socials there. Sainsburys next to the Opera House was nice, it had tiled walls from floor to ceiling, and all the girls wore caps, and the fellows wore hats when they were serving. They had huge blocks of butter and margarine and used wooden butter pats - whereby they would cut a piece of butter off the block and beat it into shape. They weighed out the sugar and tea, and it was always put into strong paper bags. Sibthorpes was a large shop with island windows, they sold ladies clothes, a little old fashioned, but good value for money. Carpenters the Bakers made lovely wedding cakes. Mence Smiths were good for ironmongery and my Mother bought two aluminium saucepans there for 2s 11d each: that would be 15p today. I have used them at least five times a week, ever since, and they are as good as new, and must be at least fifty years old.

Wagners in Calverley Road was a Jewellers and Pawn shop, and when some people ran short of money, they used to say they were going to see 'Uncle'! They were allowed money on articles such as watches or jewellery, if they left them with Uncle, and could redeem them later on, if they could afford to get them back.

Large Drapers Shops such as Waymarks or Goldsmiths sometimes employed staff who lived above the shop, one employed a window dresser, with one or two assistants to help him, and the staff were allowed a fifteen minute break in the morning and two shifts 9 - 6 and they were not allowed to sit down.

Apprentices earned an average wage of five shillings a week, and nearly always had to serve two or three years training, as a rule they wore black skirts and white blouses, the Heads of each Department had mostly been there since their teens, I don't think they got a pension on retirement.

Many items were priced just under five shillings that is why farthings were much used. The customers sometimes refused the farthing change - but accepted the packet of pins that was offered in lieu of the farthing. The change was conveyed by an overhead railway, it had wire rails which ran above the counters and contained a round wooden ball which unscrewed in the middle. The assistant pulled a lever to bring the ball down to the counter, unscrewed the ball, wrapped the bill round the money, screwed the ball up again, and pulled the lever and sent it on its way through the building to the cashier, who then opened the ball, receipted the amount, added the change, and sent it back to the assistant.

Ironmongers delivered paraffin, and you could take your lamps in to the shop to be trimmed if they were out of order. Kettles were made of copper, and later, of aluminium, but when it first came in, people were apprehensive of using it, as they thought it would poison them. We used to buy our Preservene soap at the ironmongers and blue bags to keep the washing white. Our Acme wringer on a stand came from there, as it replaced the old iron mangle. Someone would stand beside the Acme and turn the handle and then catch the washing as it came out of the rollers, which had squeezed all the moisture out of the linen. Some of the washing such as sheets, was sent to the laundry, they provided large wicker baskets with a leather strap, and blue tissue paper inside and a blue covered book with ruled paper to write the list on. Whenever the laundry man came Mother never had it ready, and he used to wait on the doorstep, and whistle a tune from 'Charmaine' called "I wonder why you keep me waiting, Charmaine . . . quite in vain?". To this day if I ever hear that tune I always think of the laundry man.

Playing Cards were sold with very plain backs, if cheap ones, but the better ones were French, and had some very rude pictures on them! Most people kept a family album as well as a family Bible, some of which had a musical box cylinder in the back and played tunes. We used to buy Stephens ink in jars, blue, black, red or green; we used relief pen nibs and we always had to lick the nib the first time we used it to make the nib write properly. Blotting paper was white, and fountain pens, Watermans, had gold, or gold plated nibs, and they had to be filled up with an ink dropper. Dinky pens were not very popular except for children, as they were small. Rulers were round black wooden ones, and we always used paper knives to open our letters.

R. W. WEEKES,

High-class Tailor

and Breeches Maker,

LADIES' TAILORING.

12, Grove Hill Road,

Tunbridge Wells.

WALTER C. RAISWELL LTD.

KENT
COUNTY
STORES

Telephone 186.

Mount Pleasant,
Tunbridge Wells.

Branches

27, Grove Hill Road, Tunbridge Wells. Phone
Pembury, near Tunbridge Wells. Phone
1, Chapel Place, Tunbridge Wells. Phone
Frant, near Tunbridge Wells. Phone

Established at
41-42, WEST ST., BRIGHTON, 1840.

MAYNARDS
FOR PURE
SWEETS.

Tunbridge Wells Branch:
9, Mount Pleasant,
Opposite . .
South Eastern Railway Station,
and . .
54, The Pantiles.

Specialities—
Perfection Toffee and Coffee Walnuts, as made at the White City, Crystal Palace and other Exhibitions.

Over 160 Branches in all principal Towns in England, including
BRIGHTON AQUARIUM, EASTBOURNE PIER, BRIGHTON WEST and PALACE PIERS, Etc.

FACTORY:
81, QUEEN'S ROAD, :: BRIGHTON.

FASHIONS
&
FURS

INDIVIDUALITY
FOR THE
DISCRIMINATING
WOMAN

DUST & COMPANY LIMITED
THE PANTILES, TUNBRIDGE WELLS
Telephone 342.

Chemists - small private chemists had lovely fittings to their shops, nearly always mahogany fitted shelves, with small drawers in rows from top to bottom. The name or names of the contents were in gilt on a black background for example - herbs - spices etc. High up on the shelves they had huge bulbous shaped bottles with glass stoppers filled with coloured water or essence, a different colour in each. They also had tall, large white round china jars with thick gilt lids, and printed in gilt crossways the name of the contents, or even the name of the Chemist. Counters all of glass, with mahogany edges, chairs beside the counter which were bentwood ones and dusted twice a day. They had a large weighing machine with a rubber mat to stand on, and a tall arm which extended above, with weights on it which moved along the rod, until it balanced one's weight. You were given a folded card with your weight on it in stones (14lbs), pounds and ounces (16oz = 1lb). They used a pestle and mortar to grind the pills into a powder. We used to buy Ashes of Roses perfume, and Ashes of Violets, very strong smelling - and very cheap for young girls. Oatine face cream which was in a shallow round silver coloured tin, the cream being white and very light weight. We used Pond's face cream as well, which was in a white jar with a pink lid. We bought compressed powder for our handbags like pages in a book which we tore off and rubbed on our noses, it was called Papier poudré. Amami shampoo, they used to advertise it, and say "Friday night is Amami night", and Shem el Nessim face powder. We used Gibbs toothpaste, and if we were bilious, we used Eno's Fruit Salts, or Kruschen Salts. There used to be an advert for Kruschen which showed an elderly gentleman in pyjamas with a night cap on, having taken his dose of Kruschen Salts he was vaulting over the banisters on the staircase and the caption was "He's got that Kruschen feeling"!

Hairdressers - when we were small we didn't go to the Hairdressers, my Mother used to put a pudding basin on top of our heads and cut round it. When we were a bit older, she had a pair of clippers very like the ones they used to clip horses' coats, and used to use those. When I matured and was aged about seventeen, I had my hair Marcel waved, it cost 1/6d every three weeks, and the assistant used to use steel curling tongs and heat them up on a small methylated spirit stove. Later on she used a gas ring instead, I had it done like that until I was twenty-two years old, and then permanent waving came into fashion. I was recommended to a Hairdresser who won a gold medal for doing them, but it was a complete failure, it went wiry all over, and couldn't be combed. I had to have it cut off as quickly as possible, it took two years to get it back to normal. Men always seemed to go to the Barbers, there was a striped pole hanging up above the door to let you know that it was a Barbers. If the customers had a shave as well, the Barber used a cut-throat razor.

Carpenters - Carpenters and Joiners as they were called - had to serve a long apprenticeship. and when qualified they were really expert. To qualify, they often had to make a miniature chest or piano or such like, it had to be to scale, and identical to the original - these items later became collectors pieces and were known as Apprentice pieces. I once bought part of a four poster bedstead and the Joiner made it sectional, although it was a Tudor one, so that it could be portable if removal was necessary - he copied it exactly.

Dressmakers - They were plentiful in days gone by, and reasonably priced too. I was fortunate enough to have a parent who was an expert seamstress, so we never had any problems, but I certainly do nowadays. It is like looking for gold dust to try and find a Dressmaker, and then they are often exorbitantly dear when we find them. The material in days gone by was of beautiful quality, especially suitings and cloths, as well as silks and satins, nearly all skirts and things were lined, and some inter-lined; this applied to curtains as well, and the velvets were gorgeous. The only concession I make to today's fabrics is that they do not crease very much, whereas most of the Jap silks and locknits had to be ironed. Lace was especially fine, as it was hand-made and there was a great variety to be had in trimming hats. Feather boas were worn in the evenings, and capes with real ermine tails on them. The watered silk and moirés were superb, and real fur often trimmed winter coats, collars and cuffs.

Food - We ate very filling food, such as roly-poly pudding, spotted dick, apple dumplings, steamed puddings, trifle, bread and butter pudding and pancakes. Meat was best quality - and our Butcher, Mr Ashby, used to say when cutting it off "It's as tender as a woman's heart". Sausages were home made, and rabbits and geese were very popular. Bread was baked in coal ovens and coal fires were in general use. We often made our own sweets sometimes: coconut ice, peppermint creams, Turkish Delight, fudge and toffee. Quite often the toffee wouldn't set, and we had to use a spoon to scoop it out of the tin, semi - liquid and quite stringy!

People used to smoke quite a lot, cigarettes and pipes being popular, the men smoked W.D. & H.O. Wills, and ladies De Reszke, and the workmen bought Players Weights and Woodbines, and sometimes rolled their own cigarettes. Ladies often used long cigarette holders, they only really started to smoke after the first Great War.

Clothing - It is interesting to compare how people were dressed. Men wore tailored suits in checks or plain dark colours according to their work, if check, the hat or cap matched, caps and grey flannel trousers and short socks often hand-knitted. If shop bought, they had an arrow up the side called a clock. They wore elastic braces to keep their trousers up, and some older men wore a watch and chain, but not younger ones. They carried their keys on a gold chain which was attached to the waistcoat button, and was called a snake chain. Men often wore white shirts with a starched collar and cuffs, and sometimes they wore paper collars to save the laundry, as they could be thrown away after use.

Evening Wear - men wore black suits with stiff-fronted shirts, they called them boiled shirts, which had a stud at the back of the collar, and wore cuff links at the wrist, black silk socks, and black patent shoes, white silk handkerchiefs, and if formal, a tail coat and white tie, otherwise it was a black one. They looked very smart with black cloaks lined with red or blue, opera hats, which were collapsible. For daytime use, they used silver topped walking sticks, umbrellas with thick cane handles called a 'Wangee': spats, which were made of grey flannel, and buttoned up at the sides, or leather gaiters.

Little Girls up to sixteen years of age for School wear had serge gym slips with braid girdles, black lace-up shoes, black woollen stockings, Liberty bodices which were with suspenders, woollen or cotton vests, navy blue fleecy bloomers with elastic at the legs. In winter they wore serge round hats like a cap, with the School badge on the front. In summer we wore on Sundays tussore silk dresses trimmed with pale blue, straw brimmed hats, with a pale blue ribbon band, white cotton gloves, and striped blazers. For nightwear we had striped pyjamas made of flannelette, and Mother always bought them from John Barkers of Kensington, they were kept in a nightdress case on our beds. Dressing gowns of camel-hair or pink fabric, with corded girdles. For day wear - trench coats like Burberrys, brown belted: in winter, Wellingtons. For dancing classes - short dresses with short sleeves, mostly trimmed with fur or swansdown, and made of silk or satin with tucked bodices.

Schoolboys wore grey flannel suits - if they were senior boys, with long trousers - and the school striped silk tie, cloth caps with the school badge on them and blazers with the badge on the pocket. Younger boys had short grey flannel trousers. For Cricket, they all wore white shirts with white cable stitch V necked pullovers, white long trousers, white shoes and socks. They wore trench coats and grey or black socks in winter, their coats were belted, and they also had grey V necked pullovers of fine cashmere - not hand knitted, woollen gloves generally navy, and black shoes. In wet weather boys wore Sou'westers and capes.

Ladies Wear - They wore rayon stockings, silk ones came in about 1928, and were mostly cream, but Lisle ones (cotton in texture) were before silk ones. Court or flat shoes, costumes with plain tight skirts, sometimes they wore a white rose pinned on the lapel of their coat, a two string pearl necklace, white frilled blouses, small cloche hats, some having small feather aigrettes on the side. Furs were worn, stone-marten or fox, which wound round the throat and hung down the back of the shoulders, fur coats Broadtail, pony skin or musquash. Crepe de chine underwear, camisole and knickers all lace trimmed, and a bust bodice and boned stays for older women, but suspender belts for younger ones. Mackintoshes often had a satinised finish, gloves were mostly suede, hogskin or chamois leather. On winter coats fur collars were worn, and galoshes as over shoes in wet or snowy weather, they were made of rubber, and were ankle length.

Evening Wear - dresses with pointed hems, and made of silk georgette or chiffon with beaded embroidery - pink silk stockings, satin shoes dyed to match the dress, hair band, and long strings of beads, for this was the age of the Charleston. On the pictures they were advertising Pears soap with Pears beautiful lady, and Ovaltine with the song "We are the Ovalteenies". Shawls were worn upon arrival at a dance or party and were made of silk with a long fringe, and sometimes had embroidery on the shawl, and were worn triangular-wise. Choker necklaces were worn, bangles and gold link bracelets with padlocks on them were very popular for adults, and coral necklaces for children. On winter nights indoors, ladies wore suede moccasins lined with real fur. Gloves were always worn or carried whenever out of doors, long ones for evening of white doeskin, never cotton.

It was at this time that we bought an HMV portable gramophone, it had a metal horn on top and we would wind it up, and put the disc on. We were each allowed to choose three tunes: my brother chose Gilbert and Sullivan operas: my Mother had 'In a Monastery Garden', 'Trees' and 'The Maid of the Mountains'; my sister had 'Charlie Kunz selection', Paul Robeson's 'Old Man River' and 'The Dance of the Paper Dolls'. I chose 'The Laughing Policeman' and Stanley Holloway reciting 'The Lion Ate Albert' and 'Please'.

This was June, and the time when the Derby was due to be run, and a man used to appear on the Pantiles and said he could give people the 'tip off' as to who would win the Derby. He wasn't a young man, he had a brown face, fairly wrinkled, and looked like an Indian. He said his name was Prince Monolulu; his feather head dress reached from his head down to his back. He used to say "I am Prince Monolulu, I can tell you which horse is going to win the Derby", he expected everyone to put money in a saucer which he had on the ground; he took a lot of money. When he died it was in all the London papers as he was so well known.

The Gypsies used to come into town and stand outside Woolworths, selling cowslips and kingcups, we always used to wonder where they got them from as we could never find any, and we liked those very much. They used to call at the door, and have pegs which they had made for sale. They also had flowers which they had made out of turnips and dyed them, and they looked just like tulips. They sold white heather on the Pantiles where there were lots of people about, as the Pantiles was very popular, and in the summer was quite crowded, there were plenty of iron seats for people to sit on.

I think it's worth mentioning a few names of people who were living in the town at that particular time, although I only knew some by name, I also knew some of them personally, and feel it would be nice for their present relations to hear them mentioned, I would stress that to me they are only past names, so that I am not prepared to say, and don't even know, how they turned out when they were older, for richer or poorer, honest or dishonest!

So here goes:

The Robinsons	Otto Dunkels	Van Meter
Barton	Perkins	Snelgrove
Castelotte	Gardener	Aplin
Wood	Grabham	Thomas
Buck	Weller	Hatherall
Honey	Walker	Franks
Spackman	Joiner	Simmonds
Cotterell	Fox	Adams
Fenner	Parrott	Spender-Clay
Armstrong	Charlesworth	Burn
Benoy	Treble	Harrison
Sallis	Mansfield	Buckland
Nicholls	Skilton	Rawson
Tebitt	Champion	Mottram
Bellamy	Oliver	Lewis
Smitherman	Durtnall	Parnell
Pollington	Duncan	Friend
Russell	Field	Baldwin
Chappell	Maddock	Gilberts Removals

Wolvey the Carrier, a most obliging man.
Cokers, White Bear, High Street.
Ginger Dunn, very pretty girl.
Louis Knowers, Hairdresser, Maison Arthur.
Old Mr Weekes, loved the shop and was there to the end of his days.
Ivan Haxell, killed in the War I believe.

Beadle	Pownall	Joan Woodger

B Chalkin
Iva Lyle, married Mr Jones, died since then; a very kind person.
Mr Pearmund, Snr, Dentist, a wizard with teeth.
Irene Chatfield, friend of my sister.

John Bawtree
Hugh Reynolds
The Taylor Twins
Miss Killick, Matron
Josephine Beddoe
Miles
Madame Adele Crabtree, teacher of languages, especially French.
Miss P E F Thesiger, TD, a leading light in the Conservative Party and former Mayor.
Mrs Glanfield, a smart and beautiful lady, twice Mayoress.
Mr Peate
Mr Tully
Dr Storrs
Dr Chisholm
Dr Hosford
Dr Selby Green
The Rev T C Bewes, Vicar of St Johns Church.
Keith Hetherington
J White
M Bennett
E Marchant
J T Levings
Maurice Wilson - good at sketching.
Alban Gall
Israel Silberberg
John T Casterton
Howard White
J Scales
Rose Cheesman
Winnie Fooks - daughter of Tailor.
Vera Cheesman - farmer's wife and lovable person.
D Armstrong
Joan Toop
H J H Hinskens
N & T Gay
Z Wilkinson
Burgiss
That is all I can recall at present. I hope they have brought back happy memories to some of you.

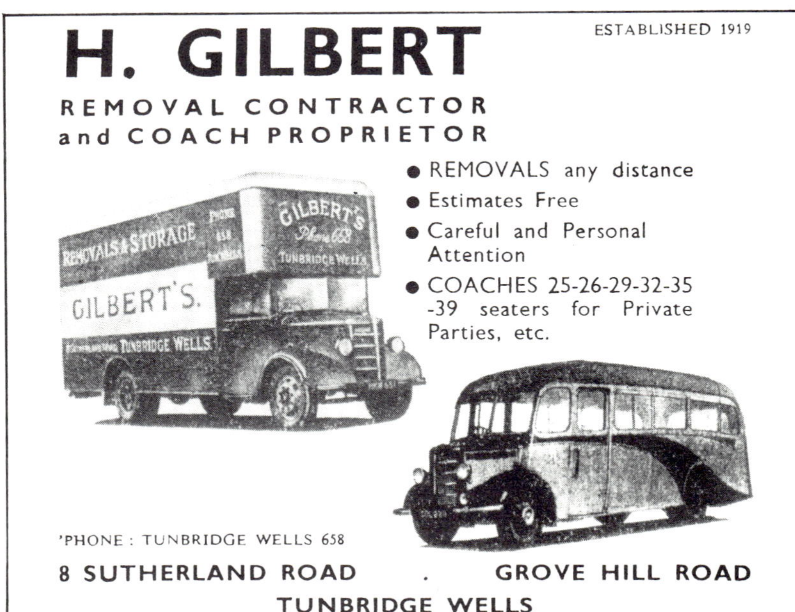

Gilberts Removals and Coaches.

CHAPTER ELEVEN

ART SCHOLARSHIP · DRIVING WITHOUT LESSONS

Time marches on - and we were all getting older - my Mother had sold the house in Claremont Road, and we had moved to St John's Road. I'd left York House and returned to Boarding School, as I found after six months away from it that I missed my friends. It was a disappointment when I was put in a bedroom with two girls, one of whom was a stranger, whereas I had always been with the same one before.

My sister had left School and taken a Secretarial post in London with a Publishing firm, and my brother had also left School and succeeded in passing his Examinations for entrance to the Royal Military College at Sandhurst. Mother meantime had renewed her asthmatic attacks again, and they were very severe indeed. I left School the following year, and will always remember how indignant I was when I was given my sister's cast off costume to wear the first time I came out of School uniform. I wanted something of my own choice, but we couldn't afford it, and she was earning and able to buy her own clothes now, and she had grown into a very pretty girl - she was one of the best looking girls in the town.

I was glad to be with my Mother, as I simply adored her. I never ceased to admire her as she was so smart and well dressed, she made all her own clothes and loved fashion. I spent all my spare time painting or drawing, and at this time an Art College in London was advertising, and had a picture of a gentleman in the newspaper, smoking a cigar; rather like Churchill to look at. It said 'Draw me'. I copied it, and we received a letter to say that they had awarded me a free two year scholarship to attend a College in London. In those days children were not given help with fares, expenses or meals, and we had to refuse the Scholarship because Mother couldn't afford to pay my train fare, or meals out. I quite understood, but felt rather cheated, as I so much wanted to go.

A friend's son asked me to go to a Dance at the Pump Room - it was my first dance, and very exciting - there was a sale on at a shop called Corinne on the Pantiles and she had a long cream evening dress in her window, which we bought very reasonably. When Henry came to take me to the dance, he was in full evening dress, but the suit simply reeked of moth balls. We went by taxi, and when we got out, the taxi had an overpowering smell of moth balls - I hope the driver didn't notice it. There was a small waterfall in the Pump Room as we entered. It was so smoky in there, that my eyes kept watering. I liked dancing as we used to have lessons once a week at School. Later on, in a year or two, dancing took place on the Pantiles on a Saturday night in the summer, with people outside Binns and our former house; it was very popular. We also went to the Old Barn Tea

Rooms at Hildenborough, the Band used to play upstairs in the Minstrels' Gallery. If we wanted them to play a favourite tune by request, we had to pass a note up by using a long pole which they had, with a prong on the end of it, and we stuck the note on to the end of the prong. My brother at this time was wearing plus fours, and smoking a pipe. He had a girl friend, a farmer's daughter. He'd saved up and bought a Douglas motor bike, and used to take me out on it. I had to ride pillion; I was very scared when we went round corners because I thought I would fall off, and he told me to sway when he swayed.

I was invited out to tea one day at a large house in Frant Road, and my Mother had some visiting cards printed so that I could take one with me. When the day came, I went up Frant Road and found the house, knocked on the door, and a maidservant opened it. She was in full uniform, black and white, with starched collar, cuffs and cap, and held out a salver. I placed my card on the salver - she asked my name, and I was shown into a side-room whilst she presented my card to her Mistress. When she came back she said "Follow me, my lady is expecting you." I duly shook hands, and was seated. The maid shortly afterwards returned with tea; an oblong silver tea tray with teapot etc, all matching, and a tea kettle for hot water, it was on a stand. There were tiny cucumber sandwiches and fairy cakes, also muffins in a round dish with a lid. My Boarding School upbringing stood me in good stead as our Headmistress had trained us well, so that we could be at ease, with the highest and the lowest, and know how to behave and be composed.

There was an advertisement in the Courier which stated that Weekes had a two seater car for sale with dickey seat at the back, for £30.00. It was a Clyno and was at their garage in Grove Hill Road (where the present Mews houses are). We went to see it, and bought it, but couldn't afford to pay for me to have any driving lessons. I was just seventeen, so I bought a magazine called the Autocar, and in it was a picture of a gear box, describing how to change gear. I studied this, got two pokers, and two boxes of matches, and laid them out on the floor. By practising using one poker as the hand brake, and one as the gear lever, one box of matches as the clutch, and one as the accelerator, I was able to change gear. My sister knew a fellow whose Father had a business and a delivery van. I asked the son whether he could take me out in the van so that I could steer it, as I had only once been in a car,a taxi to take me to the Station when I went to Boarding School, so I didn't know anything about cars.

Next morning, I went to see him and he had the van ready - it was in St John's Road - quite a busy one, being the main one to Tonbridge. He said "Get in, and you can drive". I said "Not on the main road, I've never been in a car before". He said "That's all right, it will test your nerve, if you can drive on the main road, then you'll be able to drive anywhere". I drove. I changed gear. We went down Speldhurst Road, up and down hills, and I was all right, in fact I enjoyed it. I went home and I was quite elated, I had taken to it like a duck to water! My Mother let me take the car out the next morning to visit a friend, when I got there, I found she lived in a cul-de-sac and of course, hadn't thought about reversing, and didn't know how to. So I had to get out and push the car round. Next day, I took Mother to Eastbourne, and we thought the Goods Yard at the Station was the car park. It was not, we had to move; again, I had to get out and push it. After that, I practised by going through an open farm gate two or three times, and all was well. We kept going out in the car as we so enjoyed it, but were always worried in case anything should go wrong and we would not have any money to pay for it. Whenever the A.A. man used to pass us on his motor bike and sidecar, he used to salute. He was in full uniform and we used to salute back. The ice cream men, Eldorado and Walls Ice Cream, were often seen around. Walls man's waggon had printed on it 'Stop me and buy one'. Mother found her Pension wouldn't allow for petrol, so after about two months we had to sell the car.

I used to take part-time jobs as a Chauffeuse, and take old ladies out in their own cars. I charged 2/6d an hour (12½p today), and drove many different makes of cars, large and small, but managed. My sister had married by this time, and she used to visit Mother once a week and would give me 3d if I would make her a cup of coffee; but I asked if I could take her car and drive once or twice round the town in it, to keep my hand in. I kept my licence up.

When my brother came home from College, we hired a car for the day, it was in August, in a heat wave. He made me take him to London - to the Army and Navy Museum, to Madame Tussauds, and to the Zoo! It was so hot . . . and the trams were about in those days, and thousands of bicycles. At five o'clock the Maroons would go off, so the men knew they could stop work, and they all took to bicycles. The car tyres were so thin they could get stuck in the tramlines, so what with the heat, and bicycles, I had a very exhausting day. Although that was over fifty years ago, I still have a clean licence and no endorsements.

Mrs Hayes-Jackson, a friend of Sir David Salomans at Southborough, used to visit Tunbridge Wells. She was a very colourful lady, often wearing a bright pink coat, with white hat and veil, and white gloves. She had golden hair, and was made up with rouge and lipstick; I believe she was an Actress. She was sometimes in a De Dion Bouton car which had brass lamps and fittings - and the car was dark green, and two Footmen rode with her all dressed in green livery. She always bowed and waved to everyone wherever she went. They said that if she wanted to buy something from the shops she always stopped outside them, and the owner had to come outside to serve her. There was also a Mr Kindleside, he was a Clergyman, and his Reverence used to drive a carriage and pair. He always wore gloves, some said he wore them indoors, as well as outdoors, he lived in Calverley Park.

There were quite a lot of tandems for two about, and a few tricycles for adults; motor bikes and sidecars, some with hoods; three wheeler Morgan cars, bull nosed Morris, and Alvis, to mention a few.

We used to hire a car from a Mr Boniface who had the stables at the back of the Pantiles (now the Mews). I hired one for the day on one occasion, and took a friend to Horsmonden. The accelerator got stuck, we took off at top speed, and there was no stopping us. Luckily I kept my head, and realising what had happend, switched the engine off, and we eventually came to a standstill. We had to telephone from someone's house and order a taxi. The car had to be towed home, it was an alarming experience, never to be forgotten.

The most popular dogs in those days were King Charles spaniels, Dalmatians, Red Setters and Airedales. A friend had two Borzois - they were beautiful dogs. There was a St Bernard dog, it was huge, very docile, it used to collect money for Charity. It was for the Hospital, I think, and it had a saddle with a wooden box with a slit in the top like a money box, and it got a lot of money for Charity. Fox Terriers were popular too. On the platform at Tunbridge Wells Station there was a smooth haired fox terrier, stuffed, in a glass case on a stand, on view for all to see. It was there for years, we used to think it must have been a Station pet, or mascot at one time. It was rather like one which they used to have on 'His Master's Voice' gramophones. We used to like the slot machines which had penny bars of Nestlés milk chocolate, and in another machine you could put a penny in, and see into the future. Platform tickets had to be purchased from a machine for one penny to be used when either seeing people off, or meeting them in, from the train.

When we were living in St Johns Road we had a new house, I laid a brick in the foundation. It was built on farm land formerly owned by the Cheesemans and the garden was a lot of work, as it was just plain earth to begin with. We hired an odd job man to do the digging, and make a rose arbour etc, he was a funny little man, about three feet high, who tied his trousers round the bottom with string called yorks, he was everlastingly drinking cold tea out of a bottle. As soon as he arrived, and again when he departed, we had to replenish the bottle. He used to sit on the doorstep to drink his tea and eat his lunch, which was always a boiled onion, tied in a red handkerchief. He had the same thing to eat every time, and used to say "What do you think I've got for lunch? - A two-eyed steak" he said. The first time we said "Whatever is that?" and he laughed - just like a donkey braying - he haw, he haw, and his sides shook. "A two-eyed steak is a bloater, of course" he said. After that we always knew what was coming as he said it every time. He declared the onion would disinfect his stomach. Another positively revolting habit he had, was to take his top artificial teeth out, and with his pen knife he would chip the tartar out between the teeth, and with a loud click, he would press the plate back onto the roof of his mouth. We had to put up with him, as jobbing gardeners were not easy to find. He had his good points as well, except he would keep taking snuff, which made him sneeze all over the place! Oh dear - it was a wonder he didn't blow his teeth out when he sneezed.

This reminds me of a lady who used to do cleaning for us, she went with her husband once on an outing on the train, and she felt she wanted to sneeze. She put her head out of the window and she gave a terrific sneeze, and her teeth flew out! Both sets, top and bottom, so she pulled the communication cord, and there was a great to-do. The Driver and his mate came along and said "What's happened, what's the trouble?" and she said "It's my teeth - they're on the line . . . ". They went all the way along the line looking for them and they came back and said "Here are your teeth", and of course they were squashed absolutely flat. The things people do!

When Mother had bronchial asthma she used Potters' Asthma cure, and Dr Nelson's Inhalant, which was a white china bulbous jar with a thick cork in the lid, and a glass tube in the centre with a spout on the end. A teaspoonful of Friars' Balsam mixed with hot water was put in the jar, then the cork put back. Mother applied her lips to the tube, and inhaled the steam. To do this it was necessary to cover the hair with a towel to avoid the smell of balsam getting into it. After eight minutes the treatment was finished for another four hours, then it had to be repeated. This was an excellent remedy, and brought a lot of relief to her breathing. When Mother was older and had even worse attacks, she used to have a steam kettle going all night and I sat the kettle on a trivet which was attached to the bars of the front of the fire. When the steam came out into the room, the moisture helped Mother to breathe. The attacks went on for three or four days, during which time I never left her, and when she suffered, I suffered with her. I loved her very much, and was afraid she might die and leave me. Mother was unable to lie down the whole of the time the attacks lasted, she would turn blue in the face and nearly die. We became very close, and I looked after her for nine years. A bond formed between us, and they were the happiest days of my life, we never had a cross word, we were so fond of each other. In between times Mother would be all right, and we would go out together and enjoy each other's company, and life would hold laughter, and be good once again.

During those nine years, I had two or three boy friends and was engaged twice to two of the three, but was not in love with them, so decided not to marry. My sister and I were confirmed at St John's Church in Tunbridge Wells as it was not done at School. My brother was confirmed at his School.

Pocket Money. From the age of fifteen until I married at twenty six I had pocket money of 2/6d a week which today would be about 13p, but then remember, money was worth much more in those days. The only thing I had to pay for was my hair waves every three weeks at 1/3d. I did not use make up, and Mother fed and clothed me, so I saved what I could and bought damaged antique china, repaired it and sold it to make a little money. My brother used to give me 3d to brush his dinner jacket down when he was getting ready to go to a dance, as he had fair hair and it used to show up on the black material. I had to help stem the bleeding when he cut himself shaving, as he had a very thin skin! My sister gave me 3d every time I made coffee for her, so on the whole I was quite happy. I was the Cinderella of the family and was mostly at home.

I first became interested in Antiques when at School when I was thirteen. A girl in my class sold me a sampler which her Aunt had given her and it was dated 1820. I paid her fourpence for it, that started me off, and it became a lifetime's hobby. One shop which attracted me was in Crescent Road, where the Police Station is now. A man named Lewis Pierce had a Barber's shop there, and as a sideline he collected and sold Antique china, mostly Chelsea or Dresden. If he had any damaged pieces he used to let me have them cheaply and I taught myself how to repair them. I very much coveted a large pair of Dresden ornaments of a Shepherd and Shepherdess which he had in the window. They were about three feet high, but they were so expensive that it was out of the question to think of buying them. Then one day I was looking in his window when he came out, and said "This is your lucky day. The glass shelf upon which they were standing, slipped, and they are both broken, so you can have them for next to nothing." I was amazed, and delighted, and had to carry them home one at a time, because they were very heavy. I kept them for years, they used to stand one on each side of the floor in the fireplace as it showed them off well, looking down on to them. I eventually had to part with them when we were moving, I needed the money (this was in Scotland as I was married by then). I sold them at a high price but I still miss them. I used to see a small notice in the Barber's window which said 'Durex sold here', I always wondered what it was; I'd been married about five years before I was enlightened! I became very interested in Antiques and used to go to Auctions, and read books about them in the Library and I learned quite a lot that way. I also helped in a shop free of charge, for awhile to increase my knowledge. I would always buy damaged articles and after repairing them re-sell, it was a nice hobby, and although not lucrative, immensely interesting - it always stood me in good stead, because whenever I needed extra money I was always able to sell something. I don't collect any longer, and have got rid of everything, for as we get older we don't need it, we prefer creature comforts, such as heat or food, instead.

The Opera House and the Autocar Centre.

The Band Pavilion, Calverley Grounds.

CHAPTER TWELVE

1990 - PAST AND PRESENT · CORN EXCHANGE · SPEYHAWKS

It is now 1990 and the jump in time is accounted for by the fact that I married at the end of 1938 and went to live in Scotland and was away from the town for a number of years, apart from holidays spent here. Part of my time was spent in Cornwall as well as Scotland, and then I lived in Windsor, finally returning to Tunbridge Wells to settle down, and enjoy the town for good. My beloved Mother died in 1940. There have been quite a lot of changes in the town over the years, but it is still a nice town. When we had the hurricane on the 14th October 1987 the trees in the Grove were absolutely devastated - they were nearly all felled. It was quite weird really to see them all, they were lying down like sentinels - in rows. They have been replanted since, but it may take a hundred years to make it good.

We have Housing Estates, we lost the Argricultural Show ground which must have been valuable land. It was sold to the Council, and they built Showfields Estate. They housed any amount of people, they are very nice houses inside, and they have their own shops. They built Sherwood and Ramslye Estates and the largest one of all was the Industrial Estate at Longfields - near High Brooms. The North Farm Estate as it was called, was a centre for multiple shops and businesses, all the large shops seem to have migrated down there, as the space was available for large premises together with good parking for countless cars. It is all right for people with cars, but elderly people who haven't one, find it difficult to go there by bus. Nowadays if they want to find an Ironmonger in the town there is only about one small one left, whereas we had some very large ones. Again most of the Stores are 'Cash and Carry' so a car is needed to collect the 'Do It Yourself' items. John Brown's Poultry Farm which was in Claremont Road, has now been used for building, and has many nice houses there, together with its own School to serve the Community. There have been various other small developments in the town scattered all over the place, including places like Rusthall, and it has improved the housing position because it has provided all these extra houses. There may be a waiting list, but then we have a much larger population, so it has got to try and keep pace with that.

Since the second War ended 1945, the Kent and Sussex Hospital extended their premises into their grounds on Mount Ephraim and were able to take more in-patients as well as out-patients. Some of the larger houses on Mount Ephraim were converted into flats, Williams Library is still there, and Hillarys Garage moved further along Mount Ephraim. The National and Provincial Bank in St Johns Road, Tunbridge Wells, is still there but is known as the National Westminster Bank now. Canon Hoare's Memorial has been moved further back, a marvellous feat, as it looks just the same, I cannot think how they managed to move it. Rock Thorpe and

Watsons is under development, but Jones the Fishmongers is still there. Crates the Builders have gone, and C J Gange the Watchmaker and Jeweller and former Mayor has gone. W G Harris the House Furnishers is now Courts Furniture Store. The former St Augustine's Church has moved to Crescent Road, they have a modern building there: Tescos now stands in its place. Williamsons at the Five Ways has been replaced firstly by Tescos and then by Pizzaland. Pinks the Furnishers was taken over by Jones, it is now MacDonalds. Haywards the 'so-good' Ironmongers has gone, and Sawyers the Fish and Chip Shop in Ely Lane is no longer there. Dixons now has Boots former site, and Hills the Butchers (such a loss to the town) is now Hammicks the Booksellers. The Bon Marché run by Dowsons is now C & H Fabrics, Waymarks (which was taken over by Chiesmans and then the Army & Navy) has been re-built and split up into several shops. Sainsburys moved to Calverley Road, it was first next to the Opera House and then where the Cheltenham and Gloucester Building Society is.

My Mother went to see Vesta Tilley at The Opera House. In the olden days we spent some happy hours there at pantomimes and plays. They brought our tea on a tray and we had it on our laps; we could eat and drink whilst the Show was on. It is now a Bingo Hall, but mercifully the domes are still on top of the building. It cost £30,000 when it was built, the foundation stone was laid by the Mayor in 1901 and it was enlarged in 1911. The Town Hall was originally in Calverley Road but was demolished, and re-built in Crescent Road, on the corner. The Police Station and Assembly Hall are next to it opposite the Calverley Hotel. The Public Library and Reading Rooms were formerly in Dudley Road. It was a very old fashioned building, it served the purpose at the time. A lot of people also belonged to Boots Library which was upstairs in the building, at the Five Ways - no escalators in those days. The Kosmos Kinema, although now a Clarks shoe shop still has the same window upstairs and the staircase leading up on the left hand side. The Maypole, Liptons, Mence Smith, the Home and Colonial, Timothy Whites, Toops the Butchers, and several others have all gone, to make room for Marks and Spencers, Littlewoods, Woolworths and lots of other shops.

W H Smiths used to be in the High Street but once Woolworths opened up trade moved up from the Pantiles to the Five Ways more. I went into Woolworths the other day, and reminded them that it used to be a threepenny and sixpenny store, and said "Have you got anything in here that is for sale at either threepence or sixpence?" They said "How much is that?" I said "Well, sixpence would be 2½p and threepence would be 1¼p." so they said "The only thing you would be likely to get is a few sweets". I said "Will you weigh sixpenny worth for me then, which is 2½p." So they put one small wrapped fruit drop on the scales and said "You

The Old West Station.

H.M. Queen Mary visits the Pantiles.

can have that one for threepence, and you can have two, but not any more, for sixpence''. They were absolutely non-plussed when I told them that I knew someone who when they were married, furnished their kitchen for five shillings and Woolworths delivered their goods free. They had everything from brushes and brooms to saucepans and kettles and buckets and basins, and all those things, even household steps, for five shillings - the lot. They couldn't believe it.

The Maidstone and District Bus Company took over in 1935 that was when they had their trips to and from Tonbridge, (they had a war on with the Redcar) it was only a penny to go to Tonbridge and back and they were at loggerheads. Monson Road hasn't changed a lot, we still have Madam Lydia Grace there for Millinery. I came across an advertisement the other day in an old Courier which was headed Madam Lydia Grace, and it said 'Every lady who requires a comfortable hat, toque or bonnet, should see the inexpensive show now on view at the renowned establishment of Madam Lydia Grace. Millinery Specialist, 26 Monson Road'.

The Coffee Importers is still in Monson Road - they have a Café as well now. Over the years, I think the buildings which have lasted best of all have been the Banks, the Churches, and the Public Houses. They were all very well built, and they seem to have remained on their sites, except the few Churches which have become redundant. The Banks certainly haven't, and the Public houses haven't either, they are nearly all still there, and very little outward difference in their appearance. They have mostly been modenised inside. The Congregational Church is now Habitat, they made a splendid job cleaning the stonework and getting rid of the pigeons. It was over-run with them on the roof-tops, and the droppings were disgusting, as there were wooden seats outside and it dropped all on to the seats as well. The present Tourist Office is new, and near the former Swimming Baths. Coming down the Wells hill towards Weekes we pass the former Tudor Café, the former glazed upper part is still there, downstairs is a café. Hobbs the Chemists, and Dr Scholls which used to be on the other side of the road is near the Tudor Café. All the branches of Maynards have gone now, we had two or three in the town, that's a disappointment, I know shops can't last for ever, but we do miss them. We get into set ways of only buying certain things.

The Calverley Grounds was originally called the Calverley Meadow before they built the Bandstand. It was bought in 1920 by the Corporation for £9,250 from Messrs Ward, this included the freehold of the Great Hall and there was a Bandstand at that time which held 1200 people. The Mayor in 1927 was Alderman Westbrook. The Great Hall was erected in 1870 and was re-furbished by the proprietors of the Victory Theatre Ltd., it became a Cinema in 1920. The Court School of Dancing gave lessons there in 1958. The Courier Offices in Grove Hill were sold a few years ago to the National Provident Institution. The currency has changed - we have gone on to pence, and from Imperial to metric. Years ago, in 1914 (and that's going back a bit) there was a man who used to collect farthings in Tunbridge Wells, a Mr Arnold, of 34 Grove Hill Road. He put a notice in the paper to say that he desired to thank all kind friends who had helped him get 40,000 farthings during 1914; it must have been for charity.

People had to work very hard in those days, I am quoting from a newspaper again when it said 'Wanted, a good Ironer (in the Situations Vacant column) 4½ day week, for fine starch, and fine body linen. Alexander Laundry, Rusthall Common'. Dilnott Stokes Estate Agents had a house facing the Common for sale and it said 'Rare opportunity to acquire an excellent residence with possession Lady Day, £500'. A bed-sitting room costs £50 per week nowadays in Tunbridge Wells. In the Situations Vacant column again 'A daily girl wanted at once, about sixteen, for kitchen work; apply back door 16 Frant Road'. The domestics or tradesmen always had to use the back door, never the front one, how times have changed.

Weekes started in Grove Hill Road originally, and gradually extended, by taking over the Bridge Hotel and Maynards. They were the first to be Agents for Photomaton Snapshots, whereby one would pay a set price and would be given a sheet of snapshots taken in forty eight positions, all slightly different, I still have some left. Hoopers now own Weekes shop and it is superb. Godkins is still in the High Street, there is a nice Tea room upstairs above their Perfumery and Chemists shops. It has a glazed enclosure which is most attractive. The owner of Godkins, Mr Furey, is the most patient and helpful man, he is a wizard with cameras. On Godkins other side further down is the public house The Hole in the Wall, they sold the beer at the back of the premises, like an off-licence. The men used to sit in the front shop (behind drawn curtains), they also had a smoking room behind this. It was very old and changed hands in 1920. Then we had Farrers the Jewellers and Paynes, they haven't changed hands at all, and Bracketts. Then on the other side opposite Godkins is the Bedford Hotel, now called The Bedford, Breeds the Cutler have now moved, next but one to Weekes. The Gas Company has gone, and the White Bear. Another Pub in the High Street has been modernised and gone up-market, and is called Ruperts; it has a charming kind of conservatory entrance.

In Chapel place we still have Halls Bookshop which Mr Pratley used to run; The Brass Rubbing Centre on the Common is comparatively new, and was called Fonthill, it was a Forge when I was small.

Dusts, when we were young, had three shops at the end of the Pantiles (King Charles end) and then when my Father died some time afterwards they rented No. 62 and No. 64, this must have been after Bates the Builders had it. Dusts called it their "Personality Shop".

It is 1990; I think it would be interesting for the present Shopkeepers on the Pantiles for me to give a list of names of those having shops, as they don't have a Street Directory nowadays, so:

Starting on the East side with even numbers: It begins with: Barclays Bank, then the Imperial Pharmacy (it used to be Boots), The Chalybeate Springs, Fox Brothers, Machu Pichu, The Pantiles Camera Centre, The Pantiles Craft Workers, The Regency Restaurant (used to be the Cadena). A new shop called Reporter, the one next door called Troopers Orientations, Pantiles Collectables, The Pantiles Antiques, the Post Office, Langston and Sons Ltd Riding Clothes, Howards Restaurant (closed), Butlers Jewellery Shop (delightful people), Tattersall and Hunt selling ladies dresses, The Swan Hotel, The Anglo-Indian restaurant at No. 60 (our former house), 62 The Pantiles Kitchen Studio, 64 The Sheepskin Shop, 66 the Newsagent, 68 The Bridal Shop (closed) No. 70 and 72 Binns.

Then we have The Pantiles West side odd numbers: Starting with Pantiles Hadlow Antiques, "And so To Bed" the bed shop, Todd's Vintry, R D Martin the Butcher (closed at present formerly Ashbys), The Stamp Shop, The Micro Shop Computers, Andris Furniture Shop, The Duke of York, Ceci at the Old Fish market (closed), Trevor Mottram cooking utensils (formely Charltons), Strawsons, Peter Jenner (Minstrels Gallery), Corn Exchange Food Hall, Royal Victorial Hall, Bandstand, Muswells Restaurant. At the Pantiles (past Binns, where the colonnade is) we have the Launderama, Velis Café, Pantiles Spa Antiques (3 shops combined), Organ World, Out of Africa, Upper Cut (Hairdressers), Gateway Food Market, Antiques Centre (a large building containing rented sections).

So that gives the present layout of the Pantiles; the only thing is, we haven't talked about the Corn Exchange. It's really fantastic, if you see inside, I am hoping I may be able to get some pictures of it so you can see what a splendid job has been made of it by Speyhawks. On the Pantiles where the empty shops are, of course, we are having the Beau Nash Exhibition which will bring tourists from far away. I must say, looking ahead, it would be very nice (it is only wishful thinking I suppose) if, in the summer season the Band could play again on the Pantiles; because, when it does play, it's very well attended on a Sunday afternoon, mostly by local people, because we don't have a lot of tourists. I think tourists would find it a great novelty, and in keeping with the setting. Alternatively, if the weather was inclement, then perhaps it could be held either in the Corn Exchange, or in the Imperial Pharmacy if they were willing to sell. In which case we might be able to open up the Roman Baths again, which really would be an attraction. It would need an Orchestra, even if it was only a piano and two violins: a Café would be necessary, people would enjoy when drinking their tea or coffee and listening to the music. You may say that I am romancing now! By the improvements which have already been made, I feel that as it is a Spa town we should make the most of it. I am hoping Speyhawks will succeed in bringing life back into the Pantiles again. The Stable block at the back of the Pantiles belonged at one time to Mr Boniface, he rented them I think, and with cars becoming more plentiful, made use of the stables as garages. They were not single ones, but the cars stood in a row. As Mr Boniface was unable to drive, I remember when I went there to hire a car one day, having to move a lot of them into different positions for him. I thought nothing of driving all the different makes of cars, I don't think I could do that today! The Mews shops are a great improvement.

Whenever I have friends from afar to visit me, I always show them the Great Hall Building, as I am very proud of it, especially the Car Park, as it is so well camouflaged. The whole building is so well kept, it is a great credit to the town, no wonder Speyhawks received an Award for the design and execution of the work, it will be a Monument to the firm for the next Century at least.

I hope you will agree with me when I say how lucky we are to be living in the Garden of England, because that is what it is called here. We've got everything really. I mean, when we come out of the Station, we face the Calverley Grounds opposite, we've got the Common, we've got the Pantiles which is unique, and we have high sunshine records. I have been to lots of other towns, and I've never found one that I like as much as Tunbridge Wells. The coast is only about forty minutes away, and the same to London. There is a good half hourly service to London with the electric trains; a good bus service - I can't think of anything which I don't like about it. We have County Cricket, a good tennis ground, golf course, Sports Centre, Badminton place, in fact pretty well everything is catered for. The Public Library is marvellous with Reference room, Reading room, and most helpful Assistants, and so knowledgeable. We have three Cinemas in one and dozens of organisations one can join, as all ages are catered for. I must not forget the Museum with lovely displays of Tunbridge Ware and dolls' house. I am glad I was born here. All the time I had to live away from the town, when I went to Scotland and to Cornwall when I was married, I always used to pine to come back to Tunbridge Wells. I am delighted to be back here again to spend the rest of my days.

Payne & Son, 37 High Street.

"TUNBRIDGE WELLS"
(REGISTERED TRADE MARK)

BISCUITS

First made by Romarys in 1862 from still-room recipes of the days when cooks relied for fame on quality and skill alone.

The same skill and ingredients of even higher quality maintain in a 'Romary' biscuit the old-time traditions and excellence.

ONLY MADE BY

A. ROMARY & COY. LTD.
TUNBRIDGE WELLS

J. W. Goldsmith, Ltd.,

The High-class DRAPERS of Royal Tunbridge Wells.

EVENING and DINNER GOWNS.
TAILOR-MADE COSTUMES.
BLOUSES which cannot be procured elsewhere.
RICH FURS. CHOICE MILLINERY.
MANTLES. COATS. SKIRTS.
HOUSEHOLD LINENS.
DRESS MATERIALS.
UNDERCLOTHING and TEA GOWNS.

DRESSMAKING.

J. W. GOLDSMITH, Ltd.,
15, 17, 21, High Street,

Funerals Completely Furnished.

F. W. STURT,

No. 30, THE PANTILES,

OCULIST OPTICIAN,

MAKES SIGHT TESTING A SPECIALITY

Suitable Glasses provided at a very moderate price.

Opera and Field Glasses from 10/6,
Tourist Telescopes from 6/6,
Pendant Aneroids from 10/6,
Watch Size for Elevations from 25/-,
Microscopes (compound) from 6/6,
Mathematical Instruments from 2/-,
Set Squares, T Squares, Protractors, etc., in varied sizes and material.

MILITARY & MARINERS' COMPASSES, READING GLASSES AND POCKET MAGNIFYERS in great variety, MOTOR AND CYCLING GOGGLES, RAIN GUAGES AND SUN DIALS. Most of the above INSTRUMENTS are of the best LONDON MAKE. REPAIRING DONE ON THE PREMISES.

No. 30, THE PANTILES,
Next the Clock.

THE PRAXINOSCOPE & SUBJECTS.